The
Book
of Love

The Word Made Flesh

The Book of Love
Author: Diadra Price
Copyright 2012 ~ Diadra Price

BODY, MIND & SPIRIT / Non-Duality / Mental & Spiritual
Healing / Mystical

Printed by CreateSpace 2012

To order additional copies, please contact:
www.createspace.com/3900199

ISBN# 1-887884-23-8
ISBN 13: 9781887884235

Dedication

This book is dedicated to the Book of Love written in the heart of humanity.

Special mention:

Deep appreciation and Love to my beloved friend, Pat Bellamy, who devoted hundreds of hours to transcribing these messages over a period of 17 years. She watched it all unfold through years of surrender, devotion, and application.

And to you, my beloved husband, John Price, there are no words to describe my grateful heart. I am blessed and supported by your insights, patience, and unconditioned Love embracing me. Without you by my side and focused eye to eye, the clarity of these messages and treasures of truth would never have made it into the living Word found within these pages.

Table of Contents:

Introduction

*The Book of Love is the written Word of
silence's keepings, unveiling the Original
Design etched from the Divine
in the soul of humanity.*

My Beloved, to you who have so diligently studied
and searched, to you who believe beyond the mind's
capacity to grasp understanding, to you who would serve
God from the essence of eternity, to you who have picked
up this teaching, *know this*: Love beckons you.

Love beckons all heart's choices. Love generates all life
and is, therefore, your sustenance. Love teaches all truth
and cradles it from its center. Love harbors *no fear* and
treasures itself as the Divine, forever eternal from center
to center which is omnipresent Omnipresence. Having no
fear, the mind is free to soar into the heights of Heaven's
understanding to embrace the gifts of God's Love and
bring them into manifestation in earth.

Allow your heart to be the magic carpet upon which you approach the gates of the Interior. The Interior will open on its own through your intention to be accepted herein. Allow all thought to rest as the colors rest in fabrics. Allow all questions to float up from the answers given through you. Allow all multiplications of endeavors to be supported by the universe of substance. Be sure to keep your eyes open to new and foreign matters that will complement the teachings. You will know these when they are revealed.

Prepare now for inspiration to those who cling to reason as their god. A time of reason is imperative in order to pave a road less traveled into new territories of understanding. But reasons of the mind encumber what is called the soul's understanding, for each reason seeks to find a safe place to be in eternity. That is not the way it is in eternity, for eternity is about living Truth beyond the reasoning mind.

Would I reason why I love you so? No, Beloved, no! The infant to a mother's breast is drawn far beyond a reasoning mind. Love draws it there. Reason to the migrating bird never enters the flight. Something within draws it home.

Wisdom from above is beyond the mind's keeping. It comes from an empty space of consciousness where there is a portal of acceptance to what is beyond reason. Reason, being sourced from the mind's keepings, filters into your Life as new beginnings and new understandings that are precious to your current environment of soul. This is good and true, but do not reason in the presence of wisdom.

Pasteurize all concepts for simple digestion. Allow the flow of Source to resource itself from the focus given. Filter not the teachings. Unravel them as you would an heirloomed treasure. Handle with care and precision. Document the unfolding as you would a sacred journey. Compare not notes of other's fields.

Further all understanding by emptying your mind of trivial thought. Concentrate only on the ideas given in the moment and nothing more. Do that by visionary focus to the written word before you. Allow all concerts of ideas to ultimately settle into silence. Be still and allow my voice to rise from within. Concentration to stilled focus will reveal the Divine nature of all truth. Such is the teaching of the Divine–to know itself from itself that is knowing.

Recognize any obstacles as stepping stones to glory. Hallow yourselves as diamonds in the rough. Brilliance will emerge with polish. Heart to heart the treasures unfold. Galaxy to galaxy the support applauds. Gather no moss. Gather no stones. Again, filter not the teaching. Have the occupation of surrender to every established present moment.

Complications come only when the mind tries to interject its perceptual positions. Complications also arise when the mind becomes encumbered by its own idea of self. In appearance, these concepts *seem* to separate the unified field of the stream of consciousness pouring from the purity you are. If that becomes the experience, ask for symbolism to fill your mind in empty space, and as a symbol reveals itself, draw it. Focus and rest. All symbols of Life are contained within you. All symbols embody the totality of their potential expression. These symbols will attract the fruit of their spiritual teachings. Focus on whatever is received and observe as it reveals deep wisdom sourced from the Divine. Such is my Life in earth in you.

Surely the Presence is surely that. Have faith, Beloved One, in the power of this truth. Recognize my Presence as that which looks for it and that which all rests within. Hold open an empty mind and a full heart. Offer whatever is given you to that which has given you all that you have to give.

Fathoms deep is the mind of God into which the soul can swim. Oceanography of the heart is rapture indeed. Luscious is the Life to one in space–empty space, full of treasures that cannot be seen or captured through any venue. Take no thought to the word given–just read it and allow it to be digested by that which digests. I am that! Local observations preserve your time together with gifts of the Spirit beyond what you now know. Portals of readiness become the invisible protecting fields of consciousness. Rapture is the gift of joy. Species respond to the teaching, as well as humankind.

Pleasure yourself with absolute forgiveness–absolute meaning heavenly beyond the understanding. Purify the intentions only. My alchemy will solitude itself into Light and bring into focus the truth of your eternal freedom.

Birds fly freely as the effect of their matrix of Essence. Non–duality empowers them to lift from the gravitational forces of substance. Hungry are they to find the substance that sustains them. Eager are they to follow the guidance provided within them to find. Solo, they fly in flocks together. Willows bend in unison to the direction of the wind. From silken threads the spider gifts itself a home, and from the center of *your* beingness there emerges the image and likeness of the Son of God within the Cosmic Christ of the Divine. Let this Son rise. Soon there will be oceans of recognition from the tears of joy pouring through eyes that finally see.

The dawning is arising.

And, as with Christ in the earth,

The multitudes follow the rising,

For this is inherent with birth.

As you read, listen as you would for a whisper in a room of silence. *The Book of Love* is the written Word of silence's keepings, unveiling the Original Design etched from the Divine in the soul of humanity. Suddenly an explosion of wisdom and love will unfold. Grab it not, but allow it to find its match within your heart.

I adore and respect all eyes cascading upon these words. They are words being lifted from you, the reader's heart.

They reveal an accelerated new birth in this world as each heart and soul returns to Love.

Welcome to the Book of Love

∞

The Word Made Flesh

Section One

Love Beckons

Love reveals Love, expanded always,

Embracing more of Love itself.

And in the beginning as in the end,

The all is a beginning again.

More Love expressed.

Once Upon a Time...

When once upon a time it was as I am is,
Again, I've come returned,
And view myself among my own.
Hand in hand I walk as One.

Forget me not the Word as you,
Spoken from afar yet true.
I hold you as my own.
Forever I am "that" you see.
Gather me. Gather me.

Gather with your Love in hand,
And move with Grace across the land.
Embrace the peace of Christ to be allowing.
I, your begotten, am the Love in all I be.
I am the Omni Ashni of all you see.

And when allowed the Word to be
The truth that sets you free,
Life shall be harmonized,
As the sunset to the Son rise.

Givers of Love, each of you,
Is Life given once again,
Standing before Heaven's gate,
Calling myself within I am.

Chapter 1

Expanding Awareness

*The reason you may resist what is given
is because it may not contain your idea of
what has been programmed
within as acceptable.*

You do not understand a journey that has never been taken, so allow yourself to rest and *be taken* upon the greatest journey of Eternal Life. Your Spirit knows the way. It unfolds wisdom, and wisdom unfolds your understanding and guidance. This journey cannot be gathered by the mind. Rest in peace, knowing all is well, and trust what is lifting. Do not hunger or thirst. Do not crave or regret. Do not climb or crawl. Trust! Trust from trust itself, period.

Lovingly, penetrations of the tourmalines of the mind come together to reveal more jeweled–faceted ideas. Programmed realities no longer conceal what is within, empowered by the brilliance and the radiance of the Light. And that which is gathering with you more strength to unfold itself begins a new journey in you. Be aware as you open your mind to realize what is being given here is not of the past. It will not sound the same, nor feel the same, nor be the same, for it is not the same. It is the gift of the holy energy of what is calling its name Love.

There will be teachings coming from realms beyond what has been given in the earth, and those of you ready to receive *these* teachings will be in a classroom aside. The teachings shall be given one by one. Some of you are of eagerness to hear, and some are not ready. It is neither here nor there for you to decide for others–only for yourself. Let that which is the opportunity bring itself to *you*. Behold, I stand at the door and knock, and the welcomed guests multiply as seekers to what is sought.

The faster you can understand the empowerment of your willingness to receive, the more inclined will be your mind to be willing. Fix your mind to receive as though an empty seed which is totally filled with the Light of Christ. Your energy fields will automatically flow freely of *that* which is flowing freely.

Willingness to be open to this message enables information to be filtered down into your soul, and the glory of the Divine remembered is the pure Essence of the Divine. Motivation to understand is your desire, and the Master within you seeks to bless you with that prayer answered.

Your understandings have come a long way in progression, enfolding and unfolding, revealing, even concealing until now. And so, as you recognize what is being unfurled within, the Truth shall set you free.

Do not seek to understand, but *allow* what is given to flow through, to be what it is, and to consume all into itself as one. Breathtaking is that which is giving its Life as you.

You are not all of equal awareness, so to speak. Some of you have not reached the complete awareness of unionization. Therefore, it may not be an easy time for you, but it is a time which has been prophesized by the Divine that is equal in the heart of all. Be patient, sweet one. You are being infused and defused as the Love of Christ emerges to your awareness. Remember a great truth: The first may be last and the last may be first. These are quantum times for all and especially the pure in heart.

You may feel as though a drifted child at times, but know you are not. You are within the womb of the Divine Mother, carefully tended by Love, attuned to the heartbeat and the eternal cord which connects you with the silver lining in the heavens above. You are with the child that is the gift, and the child is with you gifted. So be ye understood now: You are the child of the most high, a Divine Love–Being in the earth, united with the world in which the Divine lives itself as you.

In the Mother's heart of the Divine, you rest in the energy of Light as a child which is being birthed anew. Allowing that energy to filter through what is perceived, the membranes of the mind give way to new Life. You assist by simply allowing. Resist not. Breathe deep.

The holy Mother gathers in her arms the children of old. You are that–sent upon the earth again to reclaim the purity of innocence from which you have been called into expression. Each hour gathers me unto myself as you remembered, quickened like a flash of Déjà vu. Allow the Light, which is the Word made flesh, to awaken what is given you to be known in all remembered.

The Spirit of the Divine within you is that which is giving birth to itself as a new being in Christ. You will not recognize yourself, for you will not be the being of *be–fore*. You will be that which has emerged, eternal in the Love of God, knowing and receiving *your* gift to serve. You will not question your gift, for you will know it to be the glory of the Divine.

Trust all that is received to be the gift of the Divine revealing itself. Fix your mind steadily upon the Presence, the One, the holy energy of the Immaculate Conception, meaning the purity of the Presence of Eternal Life breathing itself as you.

Fix your mind as you would a single thought, and let your focus be of One. Help yourself understand, here in the One is contained the all, revealing the all *as* One. Numerically speaking, all numbers and all life exist within the One. I am Om Aum. I am the all in all, the love, the wisdom, the power and the strength, the guiding Light that is coming forth, and the Spirit of the knowing mind within you to guide you to what is known as One.

Currents of Light flow freely through your temples. Powerful energies flourish. Be not afraid or alarmed, but understand there is a movement of the Light of the Divine returning the mind to itself to be recognized as Oneness. The Love of the Divine filters through, pouring forth energies of Oneness to be made known. You are the Immaculate Conception of design as the Life of the Divine and the design which has come to believe, to understand, and to know that which giveth the design is Love.

"Humble" is the word for your heart which is opening, and the filtering systems within you are gathering greater strength. Empowered by your own faith, you have reached a point where you can understand what is happening is a great gift. It is the reconciliation, or the return of the Christ, made known to you through giving itself as the truth of itself. And the holy Light multiplies its wisdom teachings.

Fragrance of a dream is often the theme of the heart that grasps, as doth the breath the next one. Fragrance of a dream feels as though it is not known. It is not that it is not known, but that it is the fragrance of a dream, and so it passes by. The fragrance of the eternal dream of what you are makes itself known in you always.

Spirit would have understanding come to Light and reveal the dream to the dreamer. Each of you as my Spirit is a dreamer. It is the dreamer within the dreamer I am. Have you ever seen the small dolls which carry within themselves small dolls, which carry within themselves small dolls–each of them a smaller version, yet alike, contained within? Such it is with my Presence of the Divine in you.

Let the pastures in the future be–getten of that which is the begot, and hold not what is *thought* to the mind to receive, but *allow* as a field being fertilized by the Divine, given unto the seed contained, given unto the you, and returned again to the seed of Life in all.

Let that which is given you to give *be*. Trust it and allow your *heart* to reconcile all that is given. Should you resist what is given, the gift will be returned to that from which it was gifted. Let this be the beginning of your understanding of how to receive. You will find what is given you is equal in measure to that which you have called forth from your own heart. If you are not in alignment with what is given, you will resist it. The reason you may resist what is given is because it may not contain *your idea* of what has been programmed within as acceptable.

Lovingly, the Presence of the Light of God is heralding down from on high the light of Truth. The Master teacher within you holds the Light and gifts you with the Spirit of the Will of God. It knows only One from the matrix of itself that *is* One. As you open more fully to the release of the energy fields that can attract those energy fields from on high, you will be understood more within yourself.

Christ is a gift of Life energy, and that which is *your* desire–to be more Love expressed–draws this energy forth so you can, within yourself, acclaim it as the gift already received. Be still and allow the mind to rest. I call myself in each that is you to these gifted frequencies of messages from on high. You are to become more energized by the power that is given through them as you carry them forth in your own life. Those of you who are willing to realize you do not know anything about what is to come will be the ones who understand in the future, for you are the filters that are clear enough to receive.

The Love of the Divine filters through all that is concerned with the mind. And the holy energy which you feel in these times, though it may be confusing to your understanding, is within the Divine Light, drawing it forth and with it the greatest gift on earth, Divine Love. This Love from on high infuses itself in pure form with the Light which is gifting itself to these pages.

The filtering from on high will not have within itself corrective measures to be corrected, but a filtering system which is Divine, opened by the Light itself to currents of energy which flow freely without any thought. Allowing these energies to come will be of great benefit, but there may be times when you do not understand and feel like you are sliding. Do not be alarmed. These are wonder–full times when the Divine is expanding awareness. Simply be the innocent, which you are, and know that what is being gifted is coming forth for revelation. It is an opportunity for you to become more realized within yourself so you can feel more of the union of the all in all and feel the power of Love. Love expands itself beyond what is contained within your human mind.

The Master teacher rises within those of you who are willing to consciously be remembered as the Love you are. Only in *this* way can unionized ideas of self come to serve the Self in all. And the power from on high shall gift you with the realization of the Immaculate Conception which your heart contains so that you will understand and know you are the Love of God.

Surely the Presence washes clean the heart of one who seeks such. Make all opportunities be forever loving to all you encounter as you flow in the presence of the Presence of those before you. To all who come to the Presence there will be the Presence come unto you. Make sure your Love flows from pure intention and not for self–getting. Allow others their freedom and do not sit upon their dreams.

These teachings are soon to become the gift of the salt of the earth, and the mastered ones will understand their brilliance, and the simple ones will understand their mysteries as being the call within themselves to understanding. My simplicity is the deepest wisdom known. Let not your hearts trouble in any way, but rejoice in the given Word as the Love of the Divine you are.

Slowly, move deep into a space of returned remembrance where the Divine rests within its own design. Let your

mind be still and be drifted by the Spirit. Allow the thought
to rise momentarily: The Love of God I am.

Now focus on these words:

*The Love of God I am, and wisdom reveals its
equal to be realized in me. The power from on
high abiding within me surfaces.*

*I believe in the power of the Eternal Life of God
to take my mind and cleanse it with its power of
wisdom and Love within me. Knowingly, that which
is within me makes itself revealed and occupies all
space of remembrance. I am freed, and I am lifted.
I am speedily returned to the awareness of the One
I am in the all in all.*

*Fragrance of a dream remembers the sweet voice
of Spirit and takes me unto itself to the innocence
I am. Keeping with the idea of stillness in my
heart open wide, the gift of Spirit is free to reside,
drawing forth the Divine of Love inside.*

Chapter 2

The Return

The old was the way of karma,
which is now passing.
Behold the new, as the way
of Grace has come.

Never before have so many sought to be remembered in the peace pastures of holy Love, energized by that which you already are–the Love of God. Also, never before have so many of you sought to *understand* what is occurring, for never have you felt energies moving in such rapid acceleration.

The Divine, which birthed its Life as your being, comprehends only the path of Love which it has followed all along. The mind will not understand what beckons you so strongly to the center of Love that is now drawing you to what is called "the return or the attunement," but be assured the Love of the Divine pours forth crystal Light to all in this *drawing*. Light waves span the globe from this released elixir of Love and are multiplying exponentially. They are reported to "open the soul."

Rapidly approaching is the long–prophesied awakening, "in the twinkling of an eye." This awakening is being activated by a certain degree of collective awareness which has risen to the level of the Divine, no longer limited by collective content within the mind. The mind of humanity *effects* karma. The Divinity of humanity *affects* Grace, which gives birth to Love *re–membered.* Herein there is Love as affect in manifestation.

The return of Christ consciousness in the earth is this particular generation's movement toward the return to Love revealed. And as designed, it is to gather companionship in the union of souls. Each participant shall gather more of the immaculate return and therefore be gathered in circles of communion to be gifted with greater understanding, harmony, and love–not only for your soul, but for your regenerated cosmology as well.

This is a period of the immaculate birth. It is your freedom's song in your heart giving itself to Life. It is the return of Christ in earth in all.

Let this be your awareness:

> *I am the Presence of Light. My Light shines forth as a beacon. I see the beacon within my own, and I follow my own Light. I have a view of all earth from the center, and a view of Heaven from above.*

*My will is identified with the will of God. I accept
only what is the straight and forward path, for I
know it is petalled with the roses of Life. I am the
Presence of Light, and my Light is eternal.*

Love returns as golden birds that migrate coming home.
Love returns. It knows the way. It is the path of the soul
inherent in the heart of the winged one within you. With
Love everlasting guiding your way, the heavens are yours
to soar, and the Son–Light shines, revealing that which is
in store.

In the return, all is *reversed* from what in the beginning was
the outset of Life calling itself to full attentive knowing.
In the return, that which has been drawn from the Life
of God accumulates and assimilates. You are not used
to assimilation. The mind, giving forth the opportunity
in the return, shall reverse its momentum and *still itself*.
Before, as energy accelerated, it was a forward motion of
seeking. In the return, it is a motion of *finding* stillness
now, as that which is called settles itself on a frequency of
peace to *allow* a drawing.

Do *not* try to unfold that which is returning to itself in
memory, for it cannot be a forced measure from the
mind. Registrations of the *mind* may continue to pattern
themselves after the latest registration with emphasis. Let
your *heart* be the registrar from the nature of itself, and
from the nature of itself alone. From this focal point of
awareness is all Life given and received unto itself, and
so your Life and the Life in earth begin a new beginning.

And remember, you are not alone, for many abiding beings of the earth are experiencing similar energies.

Multitudes enter into times of questions as the heart desires to understand the energies moving in acceleration. Be not surprised if reconciliations of your individuated heart are numerous as you seek to understand what is happening. This is natural.

Fathoms deep are the words of Spirit waiting to surface from the wellspring of the heart that carries Life in each of you, attuned to the Cosmic vibration of the Eternal Son. Loving energies pour to you, through you, as the Light reveals its own radiance to the world and to your mind.

The hologram of the Golden Age, consisting of collective insertions of actions held in mind, thought, and deed, gathers momentum in strength to proceed with unfolding the immaculate of what was originally designed. That which is mastered of the Love of God shall overshadow what karmic debt has designed. Many have now entered into a time of reconciliation to the Love of God which penetrates into the so–called past and brings forth a new beginning of the Eternal. This process explains the "end times."

End times predictions emerge *only* from collective consciousness, and the collective consciousness always produces an experience equal to the same. At this time in evolution, however, the holy energy of the Divine is exponentially being experienced by the collective, shifting the *content* of consciousness to the vibrational attunement of Original Design within the Love of God.

Difficult times are ahead for some. Let foreign matter fall to the wayside and false ideas rest. Angry tempers are indeed cataclysmic to the soul, be aware. The energy vibration is not mocked, and you cannot change that, but you can make a difference by simply making a change in your own awareness. For all is One and change is influenced by the all. Herein you make a difference as a contributory to what is the Divine in all.

Let not what is offered here disturb you. In the earth there are trials and tribulations, and there is sadness. In earth is pain and suffering. In the earth are memories of traumas carried forward from previous life expressions. All of these energies may not be in harmony with your soul's incarnation and are in need of attunement to Love.

The old way of attunement was the way of karma, which is now passing. Behold the new, as the way of Grace has come. The Divine unfolds its *nature* through the heart and its *laws* through the mind. One is the way of Grace–full blessings, the other is the way of karmic debt. All is now unfolding according to the Original Design of the Immaculate Conception in the heart of God through which you emerged.

This is the era of empowerment for all beings of Light, a great time in the mastery of all the Creator has established in time. With each of you, as you aspire to release and allow, it shall be given to know.

Set your intention to abide with pure Love. Filter your thought not through what is *perceived* to be Love, but *allow* Love to be what is filtering concepts of Love in you. Peace *be* the gift given through the purity of Love as that which is calling its own returns to your awareness. Herein, all fears are regenerated by the heart of the Divine and will be given the opportunity to return to the nothing from which they arose.

Fix your mind upon what you understand to be the purity of Love. Seek not to take thought, but to release a blanket of peace given from the Love you find at rest within yourself. Invoke a flow of peace to the mind as it examines the content of itself.

Never expect your mind to examine more than it can release by its nature. Never energize more than you can assimilate in any given period of sorting. Allow a time for each process to be given its space as it rests easily in what is assimilating and integrating through cellular tissue. Do not try in your mind to sort what is collecting, for many fields are afar which your mind cannot remember. They are being drawn by the Spirit at your center to come together, community, if you will, within the self to combine–harmonic convergence of Light.

Loving energy patterns shall be gifted by the Spirit to those of you who are ready to receive. You shall be carried further than your dreams. And those of you who can attest to the reality of a mountain being higher than it seems, overlooking what has gone before, will see the gifts of Spirit and the Love returned. Do not concern the mind with what the eyes behold. Be comforted by the spiritual eye that sees beyond below.

Comfort in the heart is the Holy Spirit's gift

Beyond what the mind would belie.

Feel the peace of the comforting bliss

In the Love you see, eye to I.

Let your peace be given from within–not sought from without. And let it rise above the turbulence in the earth which affects the karmic wheel return of the past. Seek to follow the "golden brick road" to the kingdom of The Golden Age. Keep your eye/I upon that which the Light would shed the peace of Christ. Follow your own internal map drawn by the vortexes of Love within your matrix.

Be not alarmed as the negative and positive come together in your mind seeking to revolutionize your understanding of the unit of the whole. The processes by which you will come to realize your Divinity will be individual as well as collective. You "alone" cannot enter into the Kingdom promised in the beginning, for you are not alone nor are you separated from any being that has been created in the life fields of humankind. Your body tissues are thirsting to become more accessible to the Light waves of originally–

designed energy fields. These Light waves harmonize the thought patterns which have scattered and skewed the information to learning processes. To each and to all shall be the harmonizing.

The power from on high is the Source of the harmonizing, drawing itself home. And each of you is carrying forth a yearning seed to be remembered in that drawing. You feel the pull, the push, or the draw. *Allowing* that to take place will gift you with a greater state of peace as the new generation comes into expression. Whenever you feel stretched to capacity's edge, be assured that is a sign of the freedom and truth being activated. Praise God!

As you gift yourself with opportunities to open wide speculations and allow new energies to fill your questioning mind, the Love from the further worlds of God's Kingdoms shall come closer to being embraced within you. Your processing shall increase in different modalities of frequency, for each of you shall find what is calling you is like the ray of a rainbow. That rainbow ray you are attracted to is part of what is memorized in your being. You cannot return to Love in any other way besides that which is written or *engrafted*, if you will, in your Original Design by what in the beginning gave you Life.

Listening carefully to what is given shall seed itself for further classrooms within the experience of the return itself. That which is the Love of God seeks to be released and allowed. Just simply *be* by taking your urge to question to the stilled love of the Love of God within you. Take *no* thought. Question not, nor doubt. You question with your mind some ideas of belonging. You question with your mind some ideas of separation. These are illusions that have become beliefs, and beliefs become your experience. There are no illusions. There are only beliefs being true to themselves. Let the mind take a vacation and you be the vacationer. Habitats of your mind can be cataclysms of your soul. Let the habitats be vacated. Allow all to be as it is, and that means *all*, Beloved–not some, *all*.

Treasured ideas from many mansions come as revelations of harmony to be absorbed by the vibration of Love within your individuation. Your return is multidimensional and synchronizes your energy with a field of Light far beyond the mind's conception of the Eternal. You move as a field of Light, spiraling and expanding this realm in which you live, as well as penetrating through veils of time into many other worlds of existence. Your return or attunements are not to end the idea of what you call "the memory of me," but to align you for future world choices of Love.

Your Love of God is measured simply by what it is and what is allowed. It will gather you the strength and the protective field of Light through which your attunements shall be safely aligned in your body tissue, your mind, your Spirit, and your soul. Say to yourself:

I am being drawn by my Spirit into my Spirit for the glory of God. I am being drawn to the Light. I am being gifted with the pentacle of faith, which is expressed as prayer answered. I am being gifted with the spirit of Love for all, and my understanding as wisdom is expanding. I accept and relinquish all thought and sit in waiting as time waits within itself for time to occur.

Chapter 3

Revelations

*There is no distance or difference from I to
you or you to I.
There is only I being you.*

Never before has the Word been spread to such an
intensity of knowing. That which is giving itself
in Love is unfolding. Layers of the sense of separation
are thinning as they are being removed from your heart.
Listen carefully now as I speak to you from above that
which is known in you.

Calling forth what is of Eternal Life in all, the Love of God
beacons for itself a pathway. Let your heart be opened
wide by what desire calls Love. What you seek to know in
Love shall be the opening, the can–opener, if you will, of
the heart. The holy Light of Christ beckons with a beacon
of yearning. Allow this yearning to penetrate through.

I rest in the womb of the soul that seeks its own knowing.
Call me forth in your yearning. Know that I am the

yearning drawing the yearning, and let this be understood: Your Original Design impulses the yearning in your heart by its nature to be expressed. In turn, the yearning impulses the desire to will the yearning forward. The yearning is the gift which impulses the manifestation of what you came to serve. If you would *consciously be* the Love you are, then that for which your heart yearns shall be given you–perhaps not as *your* idea, way, or form you desire, but it shall be given.

I love you, Beloved One. I love you beyond capacities to grasp or understand. Just express your intention from your heart of Love, and I will hold your hand. I will! I will take you to myself of you. I will. I promise.

I am the eternal Presence of God, companioned by myself in all I see. I am the continuation of your soul that yearns for mastery–your heart's gift to myself. And you, the Beloved, know this truth.

I, the Presence of Love in you, bring forth what is given. Beloved, I believe in you. Believe in me. That which is seeking what is to be made known is *all* that you already are. There is no distance or difference from I to you or you to I. There is only I being you.

Layers of time are removed. Presence of energy moves in itself, impulsed by my Divine Light. Embrace it with your heart by totally accepting and allowing it to be. Confirmation shall be the joy which emerges. Desire with your heart not to understand, but to *be* re–membered as understanding itself.

Continue to give unto what is given you to receive by allowing all information to rise and flow freely. Breathe deep as whatever holds itself locked presents itself. Love is of the energy of the locked information that carries with it the key to unlock itself.

Let the mind drop into the well of the heart which is drawn forth by desire, as a bucket dipping into the waters of Eternal Life. Within, the water quenches that for which you thirst and fills your cup. Know it is always there to draw upon.

With you abides the all in all, the elixir of Eternal Life in blessings keep. Cornerstones support the Love anchored in the heart of you. The pyramidal point of Light seeks its own resonance field from beyond to below, from above to below, and from within to below. Patience, Beloved.

In the classroom you sat before–in dream state, not beholding what the teacher taught. Do not allow this to transpire again as you sit here with me today in you, but carefully attune the mind, the heart, and the dream state to the awareness of "I am Love."

With the eye in the heart, single to the time in which you spend in moments, embrace what is given you to see. Take the thought patterns that interrupt and teach them as children to behave. Sit them in the seats of the classroom of life to be taught by the Master teacher which dwells within. Say to them, "Little ones, be still now and listen." Take no thought but listening, and listen carefully to what is spoken.

Be not afraid, and let not what is known as thought fill you with fear. I am knowing. You are knowing. Knowing is beyond belief and registers from on high, equal to the vibration of the I–dea I manifest through myself in the earth as you. Listen carefully, without attachment or investment in what is to come, to be revealed or understood. Let not the mind dictate your experience, but let I as Infinite Mind express itself as you.

The lessons to be learned are herein simple: I am One, you are One, all is One–multiples of One, the mystical paradox. And so reveals the math of old–Oneness. Captured in the heart as history of what I am–beginning with the alpha and the omega, ending, beginning again, alpha omega son, daughter–all as One.

Spirals to beauty allow the eye to see

What is captured in the heart of you as me.

Synchronizing patterns of what you are,

I hold you, child of the birthing Light.

Framed in reference of the old to the new,

To the only begotten son or daughter are you.

Welcome to the family of Love.

Chapter 4

I Love You

*Love me now as I love you, for this is the
circle of what returns to the Source and
resources the Love I am you are.*

K eep with this idea which is holding you as Love, and
trust as you move forward this is what you have come
to understand: With the Will of God as my command,
I love you. There's nothing else for you to remember.
Having told you this, please be accepting of the fact that "I
love you" encompasses all activity of Grace, truth, power,
strength, opulence, energy, and fortitude to draw forth
your Love.

I love the Love with which I love in you. *You* are the Love
with which you love in me. These are one. Gravitational
forces seek to take the mind to opportunities foreign to
that truth. Foreign matter that is not of good intention is
being reconciled each time you entertain the thought, "I
believe the Love of God that is mine is calling forth my
name in itself." Feel me. I love you. I love the Love that

is loving you loving me in all you see, effortlessly, my Beloved One. Effortlessly! In that, *all* is fulfilled. Energy moves, and these Love patterns manifest the grand design given and written within myself you are.

Have I Love you? Yes, indeed. Carry it as your shield, and herein you shall find an open door in all. The wisdom of the ages gathers with momentum, herein army's strength to conquer all. Loving one another, spill forth your Love of life upon the energy fields where I send myself in you, and I shall be immaculated as one Life in all.

Let your focus be simple. *I love you* is all the measure of any value to any thought, feeling, or action. All else falls short of Divinity, Beloved. I love you as the everlasting Love, loving you, loving me, loving those endeared to thee. All is me, and when the mind is empty, except for that, you will know me as I know you.

I – love – *you*! My Love extended through you reaches forth to touch "I love you" in everyone.. And everything of the earth takes dominion through this understanding: I love you. Practice this ideal. The holy blessing of the Divine is always Love. It moves and carries forth the energy of creation. Every frequency of life is equivalent to a measure of Love beyond the mind's understanding. You are about gathering this energy into a new field of awareness, a compassion as with Christ walking in likeness among you.

But, make not a bond of Love. Make not a bond of any good thing, but hold it in its freedom–all things allowing and accepting. Let it be as the sap that flows in the tree to give Life freely. Feel the movement of Life within your body temple. It is budding its gifts–Love everlasting blooming.

Life offers many opportunities for energies to move here and there. This is my design. Of course, enjoy. Let these energies be from the center, like a yo yo in motion–in and out, up and down, all around, coming back. Hold me, as I am held in you.

My powers are within, contained and given again to each and all alike the same. I know when I giveth unto you I giveth unto myself, and that I keepeth all that I keepeth only if I give it away. And I shall return unto all who seek to know the Truth, the same. The joy I feel in giving from the center is the greatest of all opportunity–the power from on high ascending in its own Light to remember and gifting in the earth as above. Believe what is given and understand it to be the Truth that is the connecting vortex of Light in every soul.

Above all, the soul awaits the empowerment of ascension. Ascension is a matter of growing old–in Love. Compared to Eternal Life, it is the measure. The beacons of all Lights gathered on the hills of old shine below, welcoming each pathway as it ascends in time to Love. Follow your heart as it is given on the path, trusting that Love shall lead you

to the ascension and to the Source from which it dispersed.
This is the attunement of One.

So be it with ascension minds

And heart's readiness to empower,

Knowing there is only this hour.

No other time shall be than this,

For time itself is not.

Eternity is all there is.

And all there is as begot!

Look beyond the world the eye can see,

And the farthest speck you can grasp in me.

For ascension embraces without, as within,

Allowing a drawing you near its rim.

Then, being willing to be pushed or drawn

By that which brings the dawn.

No mind can grasp in time.

'T'is a state far beyond the mind.

The ladder was placed for you to climb.

Allow each foot to be moved as mine,

By the drawings forth from Love.

Pushed yes, from below, but drawn from above.

How else could you ascend in time?

Could you possibly fall away now?

Oh no. My Love, just allow.

Pushed from below and drawn from above,

And thus, to ascend as Love.

Light is the energy of the eternal Son given to all–radiant and luminous. Captured in the mind is my own–yours. And each of you has that access which is accessing "I love you." Fix your mind on the focus of Light at the center of I, as you, allowing that center to become extended in the Light itself. Bring your heart to the Love of God and speak the words, "I embrace the Light of God within me," thus calling it forth to express and experience itself.

Crown upon your head, Beloved, rests with such lightness you cannot feel its weight. For what is heaviness in the Light? The Light equals that which I am. See yourself crowned of the Spirit of Light moving in the earth as the heart of God, in the heart of God, opportuning the heart of God as God's Kingdom come.

Wear the crown as a king or a queen,

And let my Kingdom come.

For in your crowning and in your royalty,

I am revealed as eternity.

My Kingdom come, for I am the only one,

The keeper of the secret of the code.

And I have written myself in your heart,

As the Kingdom of your abode.

Relax with the idea: The Light of Love is my gift and carries me equal as I opportune my mind to Love's embrace. Feel not afraid of anything, for nothing is less than I, which is equal to "I love you." Let the mind rest here. Let it go to pastures none other than these. I love you. Boring? No, indeed! Try it for awhile. I love you. I love you. I love you.

Time comes to pass, each day a new beginning in the earth, an opportunity to spiral in Love. Pastures, pastures, and more pastures do I spiral and guide you here and there to find "I love you," to be "I love you," to play in "I love you," to enjoy "I love you." And "I love you" is the wisdom channel of all knowledge. Let there be, therefore, an understanding that I love you *is* the answer to every dream. The power of all energy within you sources itself from this impulse, and the majesty with which it reaches forward, opening pastures for you, will astound you. Love is the power that energizes its own self, which you are.

Help yourself to the banquet table of Love. Feast, for what I have to receive within myself is the Love I give to you through you. Fractured moments are only of the mind. A heart that feels broken is only of the mind, for I am the eternal heart of Love in you–perfect, whole, complete– and within this heart contain I all and gift it to you. Feast. Practice the idea: The Love that I am, I am. The Love that I am, I am. You are the banquet table of Love. Help yourself.

Treasures from on high filter down through the energies in the earth and filter through the energies in your mind and heart. In that which is called "I love you," energy fills all space and resources back to Source. This Love is carried within you as your Eternal Life–pastures green. Be still for a moment to feel the Love of God I am you are.

Believe I am the Love that is you loving. I am that which is sourcing itself as myself you are. From here, I reservoir into effects a banquet table, a bounty before you. Believe this, my Love, and from this ancient wisdom is freedom to the mind and the mind alone, for that is all that believes it is not free.

Believe what is given you is given unto myself. Would I give myself less than all I have to give? Receive, Beloved, knowing that what you are has already gifted itself. Love me now as I love you, for this is the circle of what returns to the Source and resources the Love I am you are.

Remember the words, "Love me tender, love me true"? Love *me* tender, love *me* true, and feel the eternal I Love you. Keep with what is known to you only in Love, and tell anything less that tries to enter your mind to go away. Say to it, "I have no need of you. I Love you. Return to Source. I have no need of you. I Love you. Return to Source." It is not of my design in my highest state of I love you. Turn it away to return to the Source of Love, which I am, so it can reverberate from a higher frequency. See it this way, and you will stay within the purities of love me tender, love me true.

You are the matrix of Heaven in heart. *You* are that which *is* I love you! Gladly be what is given and received. Take your opportunities in moments and know they are given and received in equal opportunity. The Presence is now. The equal is now. The power is now. The proof is now. Say to yourself, "I know! I know! I know!"

Every sound you make reverberates through the cosmos and touches "I love you" everywhere present. It is the joining and the union, the center from which all life flows. As you remember this truth, so be I, companioned in the earth and beyond–never alone, yet always One.

I am the Presence and the power of Love,

And my Love is all in all.

I allow that which is to be,

And I sit in reverie,

Holding Love as it holds me.

My Kingdom come,

My will is done,

Equal to the only One

I am.

Section Two

Love Attunes

You are the journey

In the journey journeying, and I am that.

My sojourn is my pleasure
and my passion.

So, Beloved One, would thou
not bless I that am you

By enjoying the journey? Indeed.

Chapter 5

Grace Unfolding

*Fulfillment simply awaits absolute
acceptance of your Divinity. I beckon
myself through desire.
I fulfill myself through acceptance.*

Abiding in the identity of Love as the Divine is the gift of Christ consciousness within you–fully awake, fully empowered, and fully imbued with *all* that Christ is. Peace be unto you now as you enter into an experience of exponential transformation within this truth. Love calls forth the Divine and is your own teacher. Coming to a new plateau of Love is transformation offered from Grace.

You are the Love of God, all of you, each of you a descendent of Love. This Love, which is growing in the hearts of humanity, is about coming to a place of new beginnings of understanding and direction revealed from Grace.

The soul that I am speaks, calling forth the soul that I am in all as you, offering Love and Love alone to the multitudes. Divine wisdom flows from the Love. And, that which is spoken is spoken anew, simple and afresh–a new beginning eternally unfolding from the center of itself. Like a flower that works its way to fulfillment from flowers seeded long ago, your garden is filled with same. Wisdom teaches: Gather your flowers from the simple fields of wildflowers in the earth.

Holding vibrations of Love and carrying those vibrations into every activity of your day brings you gifts of Grace, the extensions of the Divine in consciousness. Holding simplicity is an easy way to keep the mind focused and centered upon the moment. Let the Love of God simply fill all space where you find yourself to be–no matter what the activity. And let peace be upon the heart reflecting the same state of mind. Be still and know.

God in Heaven on earth *is* the Presence of awareness in which you find yourself aware. And each of you, looking at what *is* aware, finds the gift of Grace in all. Herein, you will understand more of the unified field of the mind of unified Love that brings Grace in knowing:

I knows I am you

And therefore fulfilled,

Moment into moment,

Life into life,

Spirit into Spirit.

Be I therefore the Attunement.

Glory is that which is the Love of you, *accepted* with faith, trust, humility, and joy. Herein Love accepted is revealed as Oneness, for it cannot do otherwise according to the Immaculate Conception of Oneness and the fulfillment of Divine Grace revealing what *is*. To invoke the fulfillment, you are encouraged to hold the highest vision of your Divinity that comes to mind. If you will do this and collectively gather, *allowing* the movement of Grace, that which is your passion shall come to fruition and ultimately reveal itself.

The Love of God speaks from itself in this truth as you apply this teaching. Desire of the heart is impulsed from on high. Your love of God and *your* faith in the power of God is paramount and imperative. Fulfillment simply awaits absolute *acceptance* of your Divinity. I beckon myself through desire. I fulfill myself through acceptance.

You are beckoned to look deep into the eye of soul. And with the mind let attention be given to discovering what is given you to be revealed. Allow that which turns within upon itself to see with the single eye. Here, beholding self to Self be I, the Beloved in you, listen for my voice which you desire to find as your own.

As you are drawn to express and experience more of your Original Design, drink as though thirsty from a fountain of the living waters of Grace, pouring from within to the without, which is, in the absolute, also within. The Grace contained within these living waters shall set you free and shall set free the generations of thought forms deeply embedded within the systems of mind, emotions, and body. These systems once freed are saturated by Grace, and you shall be renewed as though a crop being fed with water from a desert.

Now claim your Divinity:

I am *the Love of God open to the Love of God* **I am**.
I am *the Light of God open to the Light of God* **I am**.
I am *the Life of God open to the Life of God* **I am.**
I am *the Will of God open to the Will of God* **I am.**
I am *the Joy of God open to the Joy of God* **I am**.
I am *the Peace of God open to*
the Peace of God **I am**.

Living truths within these statements shall overflow into the life experience of each one of you. And ye shall stretch forth your hand and partake of the Grace–full gifts of the banquet table set before you in the earth, filled to capacity with your every heart's desire. Such is the Grace of the Divine and the fulfillment thereof.

Fortunes of the Spirit are not measurable in time, but fortunes of the Spirit are the gifts I offer mine. You are mine. Receive, so I might feel and know myself fulfilled. Any gift you give unto me, the gift I give unto you, one and the same, without end. I Love you *so* much. And every time *you* Love, you feel the Love I am you are. Don't you, my Love? Yes.

Many of you have been asking the question to yourself, "If I become fully realized within the Divine, will I be the same as I am now or will I be so completely foreign to myself I cannot recognize who I am?"

You *are* the Love, the Light, the Life, the Will, the Joy, and the Peace of God, and within you there resides perfection of that creation. Your fears, beliefs, and judgments are in resistance to allowing the fullness of the Divine to express. You will not remain the same. You will be without the fears that keep you in bondage. You will be free, for you are free. You will be Light–hearted, and you will be caring–to a depth of caring your heart has never felt before, a caring so compounded you will not know the one you care for as being separate from you. Your caring, however, will not contain within it the tension of stress, the hopelessness of despair, and the anxiety of worry as before. Your caring will be filled with the passion of service and Love, extending yourself with unwavering faith, joy, power, strength, and compassion unto everyone before you. Thus, you experience a different you. So, yes, you will be different, and, no, you will not recognize the former concept of you, as you experience yourself to be now. You are not a concept in expression–you are the Divine expressing. You are set free in your freedom to be the expressed Love of all *that*!

Reconciliations of the heart are taking place with many of you according to your desire to be reconciled with the Divine. Each of you knows the power of reconciliation, and you understand the gift of forgiveness. What is given unto you as the heart's opening is also given unto those who stand before you who are a current reality of your present moment individual experience or relationship. So, Beloved, reconcile and forgive all in keeping.

Companions shall be drawn to you. They shall serve you, as awareness gives itself more to Love. You will encounter old friends and new ones. Each one being drawn into your Life is a gift of Grace and gives you the opportunity to open wide the gates of Love flowing *through* you to give unto all.

Ultimately, the Divine draws forth your attention, intention, and desire *above all else* to be the gift of Love in sweet earth. That desire rises from the Truth you are already. Immersed in this desire, Grace is multiplied, increased, enfolded, impassioned, and gifted.

For those of you who yearn to become more realized in the Divine, you may see life unfolding and not understand what is before you. You must trust that whatever is before you is an opportunity to experience the Love you are at a deeper or more purified level. Wisdom reveals these are moments of initiation by default of the karmic wheel of the mind's keepings.

Expansion of Love guarantees ascension, unleashing the power to lift out of pain or karma of the past. Expansion is the gift of the holy Presence, the Divine Mother birthing herself as the gift of Grace in you. Your heart desires this above all else, for contained within *the heart* are your answered prayers revealed and fulfilled, aligned with Original Design.

Recognition of the Divine within those who are gathered into your proximity is a practice of the highest order. It is I within *them* that comes into your Love, and *your* Love that comes into theirs, and *their* Love which comes into yours. All is one!

Multitudes are increasing. Gatherings are increasing. All is experiencing a new birth drawing forth into earth a new world. It is a new life. Be ye therefore Life, and be not afraid. Be ye therefore the gift of the Divine Love you truly are. Be ye therefore Christ remembered, and be ye therefore brothers and sisters. Be ye therefore the Eternal I am. Be ye therefore Love!

Promises are kept according to promises kept. These are the commitments written in your heart. Keep the promise written therein to *be* the Love of God. Be true to that *no matter what*. It is the pearl of great price. Let all that you are be unfolded as the gift of Love, trusting that within it is all you desire, all you are, and more.

Pranamed as bride to bridegroom,

Teacher to Master, child to parent,

This is the promise kept.

I love you!

Chapter 6

The Will of God

*Your desire to be the Will of God
is the Will of God impulsing knowingness.*

Love is a frequency moving itself to knowingness in all through the Will of the Divine. This Will is making itself known by calling all hearts to union. Lift your mind now to a place that can receive.

That which is in quest to find itself remembered is coming to a light spectrum and a holiness pattern wherein the mind can conceive its Original Design. And the Will of God, that is the Life which moves all in earth and beyond to a new programmed reality of existence, is about rending the veils that camouflage this discovery.

This Will of God, which generates Eternal Life within itself, is a mystery. Nothing in this world can bring you understanding of Divine Will other than God Mind itself, impulsed by its own design called "Will." Should this design pull away from its creation, nothing would be left–not even the memory of it would be left.

This teaching on the Will of God is to help you understand its importance.   Generations have been propelled by Divine Will into what is called "mind evolution." Because of this, you can understand why it is imperative to be aligned, contained, and witnessed *as* the Will of God. Your biology and cosmology depend upon it.

The Will of God for you is that you understand what is happening. "The new world awakening in you is mine," says the Divine, and this is revealed from the Love of you which knows this truth already written here. Allow the unfolding which is enfolding you, and allow it to be known as the gift of Divine Will written in your heart making itself known.

Blessings from on high–pouring forth from the Divine in every phase of existence, every plane of existence, every level of existence, and every encounter of Life in form and out of form–are the Will of God expressing. God pours Life, Life, Life–always Life. Such is the Will! And the Life of you expressed and expressing is known in the heavenly realms as Eternal Life.

Holy, holy, holy be the will to accept the Will. And the speed with which the Light now flows shall be multiplied a hundredfold as the Will of God revealed–to gift a world beyond the mind to see, experienced by one and all–herein a golden world awakening.

The gift of holy Light is flowing through cellular memory as quantum infusions, transforming resistant vibrations at deep levels of your soul. And those who are allowing and accepting of these surges of energy are witnessing miraculous change in all aspects of mental, emotional, and even cellular memory. Those who are in resistance to these high vibrations are suffering.

Fear is the greatest obstacle in the way of the transformation that is occurring. This energy repels Light. Beloved, hear me now. You are of the Light and can call forth that Light in all. Recognize Light in the face of fear and offer the fear to the Divine that lives within you–perfect. Let the Will of the Divine be revealed as your own to which it is. Accept it with mind, heart, and the totality of awareness.

Prepare your heart in obeyance to Divine Will by loving yourself *completely*. In order to love yourself completely you must understand all that you see is an extension of the Divine. This opens awareness of unification within consciousness. Broadening your fields of acceptance of yourself empowers you to ultimately unite more consciously with all the kingdoms of God. And then, as you view the prospective future, you will see there is no limit or time–there is only *more* revealed of what *is* eternal now.

Make a passion of the Will of God. Make it a passion in your heart. Make it a yearning with which to be united as already fulfilled. Sleep with the knowing it is fulfilled as your will. Caress it, embrace it, coveted as you would a butterfly resting in your palm, gently, freely, but not tenaciously. Think not what it is. Just own your intention: I will to will the Will of God I am. Have this your understanding: The will to will is the gift given and received by the heart seeking to know Truth and to be realized in the family of God, serving One. Each of you carries this frequency within your matrix, and the code is revealed through your vibration as you sit here and see clearly. Your will is aligning. Let it be balanced from within.

Listen carefully when the Voice of God's Will speaks. It will guide. It will direct. It will hold you. It is experienced as the Master teacher, the Holy Spirit, the Higher Self, the Indweller, and the Voice within. But it may not yet be recognized by you as you. Beloved, God is *all there is*, and as such, all is One. Via the One, your will is God's Will–God's Will is your will.

Know the Will of God is a continuum of activity functioning as a component of pure consciousness. It is engrained in all Life and presenting its energy to the field of incarnation you find yourself to be in earth. No thought need carry in the mind less than:

> *I am the Will of God. The Will of God is my gift, my Life, a component of my all. I am the Presence of this Will as I allow it to make itself known. Now I am, so be I.*

When an uncomfortable thought surfaces, speak "I am the Will of God." Bring this idea constantly to moment to moment and to moment. If you will abide in this thought–feeling for a time necessary to allow it to anchor itself, you will be revealed its truth which is designed to be made known to you. At first it will take effort from your mind's eye to stay focused, and it will take energy for you not to be away from the uncomfortable thought. Practice makes *perfect* in this case.

Allow your mind to be still and open. If you will do this devotedly, you will be amazed at what information and peace abides at the center of your being and awareness. Your desire to be the Will of God is the Will of God impulsing knowingness. There is no *you* separate from this desire, for it is God being revealed as that which is gifted of itself as you.

There is no power other than the Will of God. There is no mind other than the Will of God. There is no Love other than the Will of God. Life is the gift of the Will of God, and it expresses in allegiance through *acceptance*. The gift that is the gift in the Will of God *is* the Will of God. Seek it–not with longing, but with *acceptance* in your heart. Give it permission as an allowing you would a child to sit with you. Let your passion for Divine Will not be as something unattainable, but as that which is eternally yours. Desire it as a peace that comforts you. Desire it as an eternal willingness to be guided and impulsed by its manifested Original Design as you.

In the context of manifesting the Will of God in your life experience, consider the following:

Hold desires given to you as you would a small child cradled in the safety of your arms. Do not seek to make your desires grow into manifestation, but to allow them as you would a child to grow. Contained within the child is the Will of Divine Love that grows itself. Such it is with the fulfillment of all your desires.

Allow desires, when focused upon with Love, to grow to their own fullness and become the perfected ideas that are contained within the desires–as held within your arms in perfection a child. This example is perfect to convey the meaning of Original Design. Lovingly, allow your dreams to rest safely in the arms of Love within you. And hold these dreams close, knowing they are the gifted Will of the Life of the Divine within you. Seek not to make your desires something less or more than they are. Do this by allowing them to simply unfold and grow of their own accord. Nurture, protect, shelter, and embrace your desires. The Will of God shall bring them to completion and fulfillment.

You receive messages and impulses for action as you live as the keeper of *allowing and acceptance* here in sweet earth. And, as you *accept and allow* all that is given, all that cometh, all that goeth, and all that is, you are being true to the Will and Nature of the very Life you are that is absorbing this message right this moment.

Say to yourself:

> *I allow what is to be to be, and I allow what is to come to come, and I allow what is to pass to pass, equal and the same, one movement in the present aligned with Divine Will.   Herein I abide as the gift, the giver, and the given, and I am that which is of God, giving and receiving to and from its own— accepting all.*

If you will abide in the awareness of the above and the words of intention, "I accept the Will of God I am," you will draw unto you Light frequencies of energy from the junction box, so to speak, that will help you grow rapidly into new states of awareness. Junctions transfer connecting links of your soul, much like a circuit of electricity. The Light of God is literally beaming throughout the physical body within circuitries of strategic points or junctions and disperses itself into tributaries of energy fields and frequencies.   This is accomplished by the impulse of Divine Will.

Fish swim deep.   Original Design in the soul is deep, immersed in Living waters.   And from the sea all Life was given birth in earth in Original Design, impulsed by Divine Will.   Believe it or not, the composite of the ocean I am in you, for out of the Life of the sea I walk in earth. The ocean feels the opening of your heart and, believe it or not, smiles within itself in pure joy, recognizing itself through you. The sand beneath your feet rejoices, believe it or not, every time you step upon it, leaving my imprint behind.

Your footsteps in the water's edge am I, as eternity waves itself in each experience of life. And what shall the sea dredge up upon the shore of life from storms that come? And where would the sea take you if you let it? Explore and find.

> *And all the fish in all the sea*
>
> *Swim effortlessly,*
>
> *Around in circles, here and there,*
>
> *To find that which is everywhere.*

And such it is with every day and every moment in the day, an exploration in what I keep hidden in the seas of myself to bring to shore remembering, or new life you've never seen before, perhaps, or memoried treasures of old. Such it is, my precious one, my soul, the sea within yourself, supporting the you here in the earth. Allow my tides to be the waves of your soul and carry you out to sea/see. I am the trust with which you are trusting, as are the waves in the sea. The waters of the oceans care not where they meet the earth and land, but allow the pull of the tides to take them where they will. So be it with you, my child, and I will bring you home unto myself in every shore I take you to. Wherever you are, there I am kept as the Will of God.

Fish swim in deep waters. This is because it is necessary for the fish to be infused with "sound vibrations" that sustain Life. In the deep, fish are permeated by sound waves entering into the planetary system from on high, meaning "dimension of frequency." If you will abide deep in the ocean of consciousness, carefully attuned to the vibration at that level, you, too, will be infused through the frequency necessary to bring your state of awareness to a higher understanding of itself, moving in a new direction of purpose for the mind. Such is the Will of God.

Diving in the waters deep is a little scary to the unencumbered soul, much less to one who has encumberment. But trust, my Beloved One, that in the deep you find your Light in the depth of darkness below the content of the sea of consciousness–deep, deep. Dive in waters unknown without fear encumbered. Allow. The vortex at the center draws you deeper to itself, and here you find my indescribable Divine Will that draws you even deeper than itself.

I am the keeper of your mind, and your mind is mine. And, as a coal*miner* goes deep into the caverns of the earth, allow me to be the *miner* in you, going deep into the caverns of your soul, revealing to you gold yet to be your fortune. Come, Beloved. Go deep, deep within, for I am deep within you. I am not a "being" outside of you. I am the Light surfaced to a level of consciousness to communicate with you, *as* you, *through* you. Your Light energy field is expanding to the point where aligning with it is as easy as turning on a television set to receive. The frequency is in the house in which you live–your consciousness. You have attuned to this frequency through much intended will toward the Divine. The channel from which you desire information is available. Choose it.

The Will of God is always at the center of you as that which you are. Never doubt this, little one. Never doubt it is at your center, and from that center do you flow. When you know this, then you, the Will of God you are, aligns to bless *you* with all the information, all the Light and Love, all the wisdom, all the understanding, and all the guidance Jesus, the Master teacher, walked with in the earth.

Attuned to the Cosmic Christ level of Light and Love, Jesus brought forth a teaching that would not die because it was an aspect of the Divine nature of all humanity. That nature is now being even more consciously aligned, understood, and expressed from within by the movement of Divine Will. Do not misunderstand when I tell you, you are the beloved consciousness of Christ. This consciousness is within all beings. It is what is termed "the fulfillment of the prophecy" from Jesus Christ when He said, "I will come again, and I will take you to myself. That where I am, there ye may be also." When the Master appears within you as the indescribable, you shall know this truth.

Trust what is herein given in you, sourced by desire as yearning to know. This is the Will of God. And all things follow as you allow the yearning to be fulfilled. Accept with certainty that God's Will is the only Will, and that Will is the Will of you.

I am willed by the Will I am

To manifest myself.

And herein rested in, as that which you are,

I am blessed.

Chapter 7

Your Gift of Spirit

*Each of you has "the Gift of Spirit," and
the Gift of Spirit is unique to each one–yet,
it complements the Spirit in all.*

Coming into new understandings, you are opening
aspects of your nature you have not understood in the
past. If you find yourself at a point where you do not
understand the feelings and emotions that are rising, it is a
very good thing. Not to worry or be afraid. Just be curious.
Wisdom teaches the gift of all life is curiosity, much like
a cat would to explore its own space. Give yourselves to
curiosity and do so with the Love of God forever at your
beck and call, seeking you to find. The shift of the ages is
very much at hand, and each of you carries what is written
in your heart as found.

Your minds are undergoing change, deeply so. And your
will is no longer being strongly influenced by methods
that used to control your sense of separation and personal
will. You are being impulsed by Divine Love from deep

within yourself. Any resistance that might be experienced as this takes place will bring some of you to points of confusion, doubt, and pressures of the mind. But the more you consent to Divine Love, the less stress and more energized and empowered you will feel.

Holding you with Love, gathering you in sweet caress, the Divine becomes the gift that is gifted. Herein, there is joy as you receive what is given as manifestations of Divine Grace. Pouring into the planetary system, this is a gift to all Life encountering itself, one in the other one. This energy is opening the mind and the heart to truisms which have not been acceptable before–such as:

> *The Love of God is the Source of all that is; and*

> *The Love of God is every movement of Divine Will; and*

> *The Love of God is what carries forth its Life in and as me–each breath I take; and*

> *The Love of God is the yearning in my heart to reveal the Love of God I am.*

I, the perfect idea which is gathered within myself, am now coming to experience all in all, little by little, as though a snail creeping across the ground searching for the all that is in the earth. I have gathered wisdom, love, understanding, peace, joy, fear. You name it, I've gathered it. And I am about reclaiming my territory as the Divine, which accepts all things.

You, Master teachers, beings of Light, angelic realms, kingdoms come, all, are the Divine, holding a pattern of energy that is *so* beautiful to behold. Acclaim your name as holy, and rejoice in these days to come.

Heart centers are being claimed by the Love of God every time your mind says, "Here I am, Lord. I seek to be your Love in earth." As you move forward with this idea to focused Light, you will not be able to contain the glory of it all! You will feel so elated at times you think you might explode! And you *will* explode with joy, peace, love, understanding, and tremendous encounters of Light! Those who abide with you will simultaneously rejoice in your rejoicing.

Carry what is in your heart's desire as a small idea of a new beginning you are entering, and let that little bit of the gift you can see in this moment be as a small speck of what is to be revealed to you. The eye/I is revealing the single eye/I of the Divine which sees through the Light of itself and beholds kingdoms beyond this one. Holy be the energy embracing those of you yearning to be remembered in the Love of the Divine and embraced as the Eternal Life of God you have been seeking.

The Love of God extends itself and carries with it information that may be beyond your mind's grasping right now. But in the days to come the mind, having accepted more of the Love that generates its ideas, will be embracing more of that and, therefore, understanding more of its ideas in creation.

Each of you has spent many eons of time in evolution, and the Love of the Divine is rejoicing as the evolution blooms as consciousness that has been seeded in the past. You have gathered nourishment from the experiences in the earth and beyond. To God is the glory. Each evolutionary spiral into a new experience of life gives to the giver the gift of God *as* you, a blessing, and empowers you with more creative ability.

Registrations from on high have come to bless you with the gift of Light. And as you experience this Light, each of you will have a different experience of what that energy feels like. Movement, stirrings, and penetrations into the heart fields of remembrance are common. Some of you will experience the bringing forth of an activity of energy that is felt as unconditioned Love, insatiable joy, or even pain and sorrow. Be not afraid, for as the coming of the Christ was promised of old, so it is with you now. And each of you will have your own personal experience of blessings of Grace and Love that empower you. Hold the patterns of energy as they hold you, understanding that no matter what the energy felt of mind and heart, it is the *Divine* revealing itself remembered as you.

Each of you has "the Gift of Spirit," and the Gift of Spirit is unique to each one–yet, it complements the Spirit in all. And, as this gift unfolds into the Light of remembered union and creation, that which you create from the aspect of knowing this truth will be beyond your grasp to entertain at this time.

Holy is the Light of God in all, and all Light now multiplies rapidly. Holy be the gift encountered in the earth as manifestation of the consciousness of each of you. Many walls will begin to crumble very rapidly, and that which is of lesser light than that which is Eternal Light will be brought into the Light of defused energy so it can be re–created again in a higher frequency and dimension of space. Press not against the walls of time, but allow them to crumble on their own.

Let your mind be rested. It is the most important lingering that can be entertained in a moment's time. Hold the idea of simple abundance, gracious giving, and multitudes of information coming through. Let each idea given in a moment fill all space in your mind, and, as you allow it to fill all space, then be with it in awareness *constantly* until whatever idea enters to take its place.

Consider the lilies of the field. Are they not beautiful and radiant in their expression? Let them be your teachers and mentors. Listen to the song of the Lark as it trills to what is present in the moment. Capture the freedom in the wind and allow whatever is moving around you to find its rest. Nothing is more important than what is here now— nothing. Usher in all time as if it is the greatest moment of your Eternal Life. This is the place, the time, to seize the moment, for herein all is given and received.

Let not your mind wander to future time, but keep a listening mind to this moment in which you find yourself to be. Realize in each moment you have eternity and the gift of Spirit making itself known. If the mind wanders and roams, how can you possibly perceive what is here at hand now? Such is the Kingdom of God. Remember, the Kingdom of God is at hand.

Your future is nowhere to be found, but your Eternal Life is everywhere present. Yesterday is eternity remembered in the freedom of the now. Tomorrow is the longing for a dream already fulfilled and complete as it rests in imagining. Welcome each moment as a child to adventure and allow the future to be the now. Allow the past to be here as well, for all is kept as *this promise* in your heart: The Love of Divine Love you are–nothing to fear or dread or seek or find, just Love to *be*. Allow.

Holding you in the timelessness of time itself is the Love of God, for so–called time is a holding space for transformation. Time, as you know it, rests within the Love of God that draws you to itself. Whatever that Love is in the making, it shall be in you thus given–Life fulfilled– until such time that time stands still, having fulfilled its purpose full. Synchronizing units of measuring time, forget it. It is not allowed. Every "now" gifts a new idea. Allow each moment's gift to fill the space which occupies focus in the moment.

If you can come to the understanding that listening in *stilled silence* is a Divine activity needed for your entire being to fill all moment in space, you will be gifted beyond measure with the ability to gift yourself with what you desire to have given.

The Love of God fills itself with desire in the heart of you. And now you understand, coming into the power of One, you are a Light, a beautiful Light, a glorified Light of the Divine expressing itself in time, giving of itself to time, and being of itself as you *are*. Be still as you allow the Divine to fill your mind with information which is needed to assist in your knowing more of who you are.

Beacons of Light help you see the gift of Eternal Life. These beacons pouring into this planetary system are received by antenna, so to speak, reaching forth through desire to know the Love of God. Each time you bring the focus of awareness to this activity or intention of mind and heart, you literally draw into yourself beacons of Light.

Light is the only description you can understand that offers more of itself in what is created as you. You are attracting Light because you *are* Light. In this attraction, you become realized as more unified–always. And when the mind cooperates with the natural Light at the center of all Life, which you are, bringing its focus into alignment with the state of being that exists in you, then you begin to absorb and attract Light at frequency levels beyond your current measure. The Light then is free by that which is called "no interference" from the mind. It is free to take within itself what is given of the Light called wisdom, love, understanding, and transformation of soul.

Each of you is a participant of One, bringing into your frequency (or measure of existence) your attentive awareness. Each of you is bringing in frequencies that are contributing to the whole, making it easier for you to bring in this information through the Light and attracting it as a whole. As this occurs, it increases exponentially in the earth daily and brings about a quantum leap of consciousness spiraling into new beginnings.

You are translucent radiance as the Divine becomes brighter and brighter, moment by moment in you. By the nature of itself, the Love in the Light always makes itself more visible and deeply understood. In fact, it is about giving a treasury of sorts to the mind, so not only what you have understood in the past, but what you will grasp in the future, is more available to you now. From the perspective of the current moment reality of mind's capacity, you will be able to grasp more of what you truly are, even though not yet revealed.

I am the Presence of God. God is the Presence I am. I am willed to understanding and guaranteed the Grace that comes, which is given by Love.

Chapter 8

Let Not Your Heart Be Troubled

*Worship is the act of seeing, being. It is
the act of seeing, being what you truly are,
not what you think you are.*

L et not the heart be troubled, for I am the peace of
Love, and my peace is thine own. Let your joy be
full. Functioning as the heart of God I am you, no more,
no less, not two, but one, equal and the same. Follow your
heart always. Listen with your heart and see with your
soul, and let it be known, "That which knows what cannot
be known is of no use. Be gone. Be gone." Let not your
heart be troubled.

Mine is thine, thine is mine, equal and the same. No more,
no less, not near, not far, but here right now. All circles circle
and continue to circle, giving and receiving circular vision

to those who have eyes to see. Giving and receiving are equal and the same, one movement of Love. As Love, be ye therefore loved–one movement given and received. From this day forward, being only this day and this truth, let it be what it is, thus empowering your heart to be troubled not.

Trial and error, here and there, accept–a part of Life. Allow all life to be. And, in the allowing, vacation your mind from outer things to *be–holding* the Eternal Love I bring. No place to go, no thing to find, nothing to fix or rewind, just allowing all to be as it is. Let that which is Love move itself as does the winged bird in flight, allowed, allowing. Thus, nothing remains to trouble.

Worship is the act of seeing, *being*. It is the act of seeing, being what you truly are, not what you think you are. And every time you "real–I–ze" me everywhere, realm to realm, joy to joy–even tear to tear–you enter true worship through the *stare*–way to Heaven. So, let not your heart be troubled.

You multiply "now" every time now is remembered. Now allow the thoughts to pass as rivers do themselves. Streams and streams and tributaries dialogue not, but allow free territory to what passes over. From this to that and here to there is equal and the same, a present moment of Love. Precious moments, guardians of Life you are. Let not your heart be troubled.

Precious moments,

Endearments of the heart,

The rending of the veils to part,

I love the Love I am you are.

Let not your heart be troubled.

Give up the goal to get.

Return the Immaculate Conception,

The gift of Life unto itself. Be that!

My wisdom is the keeper of the Essence of you

And releases itself when wisdom is due.

Let not your heart be troubled.

I am the Immaculate Conception you are,

The only begotten Son.

Let not your hearts be troubled,

My precious One.

Assistance is given according to what is called upon by the *open door* in your heart. Behold, 'tis I as you that knock, offering what shall no longer be remembered but *known*. You must be willing for the door to be opened from within as an invitation to "the guest of honor" there knocking.

Be sure to give this One the seat of honor and that which is called "the floor." Let *Love* speak. You have been the householder until now. The guest of honor is the landlord, the Love of God, if you will, which built the house in the first place. Do you sit with admiration as you gaze into the eyes of me standing or sitting there before you? Can you see me everywhere and know that what is seeing is me everywhere seeing? If so, then what is there to trouble you?

Likewise, give you, yourself, to each one standing in the opened door, as I am complete in all. The gift of Love will reach forth from your heart for all to come in. A welcome mat is always an invitation to enter what you call your own. An open door is an invitation to enter into the manifestation of all within your heart's desire. Hold a welcome. Send an invitation, an announcement of your gift to give, that being my Love extended as you, as your Original Design and theirs fulfilled.

Hosting Life, always open the home in which you live to all in knocking. I am there. Precious moments, indeed, bring forth the Grace of God to seed itself again and again through the heart of Love that opens the door and through the heart of the one knocking. You are that. And in *that*, my Beloved, let not your heart be troubled.

Recognition of my own voice,

In each of you I speak.

Let not your hearts be troubled.

Accept my infinite peace.

Chapter 9

The Flow

Measure not what is the extension of God's infinite formations, but look at all there is as manifested flow of Life Divine.

Perhaps, it is time to lay down the burdens of the heart. Let this be an easy task–not a burden in itself. Learn to spell "ease" with a capital "E." Multiplied, expanded, quantumed–you get the idea–such is Life of itself, easy. But, oddly enough, release is not easy for some. Holding on to things, to strings, to bundles of burdens, often seems more appropriate than laying them down or letting them go. At least the burden is the known. "What would take its place?" the mind questions. "What would take its place?" And when your heart questions to the mind, 'tis arising from the Love I am to gift revelation to myself as you, which is the revelation of Love. It is a paradox of sorts.

The Light of God guides you in the experience of spiritual evolution. It is a blissful joy as the soul reaches higher elevations of itself through which it can see far beyond what has gone before. And each time a new elevation is experienced, mountaintop peaks come closer into view. Allow effortless evolution to be the joyful Will of God drawing you forward in the Everest climb of what is given in the space of earth to accomplish. And, as soon as you reach the highest realm the earth space offers unto you opportunity, you shall be carried to the peak realms of Love.

The Life of God is the only beginning. It never knows an end or a limit. And the pastures of Life are forever flowing, one into another one. Mountains and valleys, where does one begin and end? All is God remembering expression of itself as Oneness. Allow your Life a seamless garment to be of the soul, and return unto Heaven, awake, enjoying one plane flowing within another one, as all is that which Reality is given. Expand in this world what is believed in other worlds to come, and you shall know Heaven is here. This be unto the truth keeping: The heart remembers all as One.

As the hills in the mountains rise, so am I in you.

And in the valleys, 'tis I walks through,

Remembering me,

Throughout eternity.

And all I see, and herein again I am

One.

∞

Let mountains hold your heart

As blankets for your soul.

Receive ye their gifts

For centuries told they hold,

The promise kept of life embraced,

Valley into mountain one.

Each equal to the same as one,

Not visible without the other one.

Each one of you gifts into the givingness of life which carries forth energy of great dimensional Love. This Love is capable of sewing together the hearts of humanity that have ripped wide open, by fusing them into a seamless garment of One. There is no stitching in the seamless garment of the Love you are–full circle, complete, no beginning and no end. You have the yin, you have the yang–two halves of a complete. There is no beginning and there is no end to Love. But, in a world of finite, you always have a beginning and an end. They cannot be seen as a continuum of One, because in this world they are perceived to be opposites. They are not opposites, but equal parts of the whole. Rest as the garment of pure seamless Oneness–unconditioned Love in every thought and feeling that emerges from myself as you. Oh, how happy am I–the joy I feel. And, in that joy, I know myself as the joy you are, whole, complete, and Heaven sent.

The test of time shall be given unto you happiness drawn forth. The same happiness as a newborn greeting new life shall be your happiness. That is what graduates you into a multi–dimensional being of great joy.

Happy are those who allow happiness to be revealed as laughter and joy. Laughter is the substance of the soul, the keeper of the flame, and that which is the joy of the Lord. Laughter is the effect of consciousness directed within itself to find its own humor in life. Laughter is the effect of joy, and joy is the effect of Spirit, and Spirit is the effect of God, and God is the effect of Love.

Humor is God's *greatest* experience of itself, for herein is God revealed–indeed! Happiness is the matrix of which all begets its own idea. It is the rising of purity from innocence. Place not your happiness in anything less than happiness. Worlds within worlds create themselves out of this energy form. Rush to the energy fields of joy, the forever given in the flow of happiness.

Happiness moves as do spirals of Light, expanding and contracting. And all in happiness rises *with* the expanding and the contracting. Gift of Light is happiness rising and falling, rhythmed in you as the breath moves inward and outward, a bellows of sorts. It is holy breath in all that breathes, and as your breath rises and falls in joy on its own, happiness rises. From joy to happiness to bliss rise I, the flow of all Life.

Carry forth what is given in you to be remembered, allowing it to show you the way. Would you not follow the Light if it were there? Of course you would, and so be it with you now. Joy is the way for the Light to shine, so, when you are in joy, you know you are following the Divine. And here the Kingdom of God blossoms as a field of daisies growing in Love.

Progression in the earth is my purpose here as you, and I offer it in every breath. Breath work is important, Beloved. When you take a breath, take it with conscious awareness that I, the keeper of the breath, take it as you, *automatically* within my own control which in you rests. Breathe easy, with a natural flow, as the wind that carries the seeds of Life where it will.

You, Beloved, are the seed of Life I bring–multiplied, remembering, holding Love as the sun/Son holds Light in the earth. And though I flow within your soul as sun and shadows to the earth, I always bring a glorified morning in you. Walk away from the shadows. Leave them behind–to follow the Light within them.

Your soul, gathering momentum and strength, is now expanding. Luscious, rich, gracious and generous, the soul of you rests in the opulence of its own Original Design of you. Love beckons all into being, creating after the image and the likeness of the Divine Design. From the core of the heart of God, the soul of Love you are extends itself in earth and unfolds the wisdom teachings herein written from on high.

In many ways you are entering new fields of mastery. Mastery is simply allowing Life to fully express itself in and as all Life. It is identifying all as the expression of the Divine, knowing the joy of the Divine is in individual expression of itself. Appreciation of Life expressing in any form will open you to a greater dimension of expression.

The natural flow of Life is known as allowing the wheat to grow with the tares, and the sun to shine opposite the moon, and the wind and the rain to be together one. Large amounts of hail may fall, and yet they soon melt and become what nurtures the grass. Measure not what is the extension of God's infinite formations, but look at *all there is* as manifested flow of Life Divine.

Pastures are green as they drink of the waters from Heaven and rest in the basking Son/sun, equal measure. Overflowing into the reservoir of the memory, my elixir of Life returns the soul to the mastery of perfection as you, but you must be still. A busy mind is just that, busy. I cannot reach the conscious realm if business is the occupation of the mind.

Go often to the well of the water that flows freely in the quiet. Draw forth from this center–from the purity of this Source. Your mind cannot contain both earth and Heaven alike–you must choose. To choose Heaven is to relinquish the contextual burdens of the mind. Generations come and go, express, and retire. Let this be the ways and the means of the *attire* of the mind.

And I, the falcon, fly freely here in sweet earth as you and me. Observe with single eye/I the earth beneath your feet, and soar in Heaven's way your mind in keeping. Let freedom ring from its own ringing–the voice spoken from its own voice. The winds are wild with joy. Never before witnessed of the witnessing such as this has taken place in earth, and *you*, Beloved, are the single eye from which I see in all. Single eyed as the falcon flies free, so am I in thee. I am captured in freedom. I am set free in Love.

> *Hold the door open with your mind,*
>
> *Keep your eye single, yet not blind.*
>
> *Allow the greatest gift to be,*
>
> *The gift of Love flowing free.*

Do you understand? Indeed you do, for what is understanding but its gift in earth of me? Your understanding expands with the willingness to know more of the unknown and to journey further and more deeply into the forest of the mind. But facts do not give you understanding–only understanding gives it to you. Legacies of old empower more truth for revelation, for they serve as the foundation upon which to build understanding. Life always generates more life in simplicity, complexity, and expression to be understood, for storehouses of information await on the inner planes for revelation to the mind and heart that is open to receive.

One who listens and is still can hear the voice of Spirit echoing as a canyon wall from the Spirit of Truth. The joy of God is the voice of your own keeping and, always assured, brings Light to every situation and a lifting to every heart.

Wisdom seeks its own level of truth

And offers it as Life expressed.

Impulsed from Love is wisdom's keeper,

Too blessed to be depressed.

A wave tucks within itself in its *return* to the ocean. Anchored in Love, as ocean is the sea, so am I in thee. Programmed realities are falling away as waves to the shore. Deplete not anything with a *mind* that thinks it is complete, but rather allow it as a *movement* of one expression of Life into another. And, as the sea/see flows within the ocean of Life, my wave of Life returns to sea/ see all I see through your eyes.

Let your understanding be a wave in the Cosmic of the Divine. Allow that wave to take you where it will. Do not seek to find, but allow what is to be. And herein you will know the Truth and be set free in the flow of your mind, and your mind alone, for you are already free in your Spirit.

I carpet myself for your footage in the earth. I step my journey every moment of your life. What a journey I have taken each step you took. Follow the carpet I have laid before you always. It is followed simply by the realization that it is I that takes the step, I that guides the step, I that is the step and that which is stepped upon. All is one. I keep you always. Even when you feel afraid, I am here. Even in your question, I am here. And even in the step you take in your fear, I am here! How could you ever step away from me, when I am every step you take?

I love you beyond the word "love" does promise. I fathom myself only through you and come to know me as I am. I am companioned by the knowing and rejoiced in my expression of you. Be at peace, Beloved One. The multitudes are coming Home, and so are you.

Each of you is the Love I am,

Serving one in another one,

Keeper of the flame.

And the eye that I sees through you

Is the eye that sees through the other one.

Recognize this is what is called "coming home."

Chapter 10

Fresh Fall on Me

"Fresh fall on me" is an intention that can
help you surrender anything
that is in resistance to Love.

There are not kinds of Love. This is a misperception. There is *only* Love. Project not then what you think Love is. Simply allow it to be. My Love rests within yours. Yours rests within mine. Allow Love to flow. Each of you must find this within your own being, and here all the begotten which is given shall be made known to you.

Resistance to Love causes corruptions in the soul, leaving irreparable scars of memory in the mind and heart. Allow these scars to be regenerated by the elixir of Divine Grace, for to try to heal memory at the level of the remembered will, by the law of attraction, create more of the same. Grace remembers only what is true to Love, and, when all memories are surrendered to Divine Grace, by its nature Grace regenerates the "irreparable" to reflect Original Design.

Most of you have encountered many struggles along the way that have left memories that are resistant to Love. Please do not be dismayed by this information. Realize instead that struggles can lead to a deeper realization of Love. Bring your struggles to the altar of your heart, offering them up to the Divine of you. Trust what is given you to remember on a daily basis of woe, as well as a daily basis of Love. Trust what is given or revealed is from your Divine Spirit to help you see what is in resistance to Love and what is in alignment with Love. And if you would be "multiplied in Love," cradle Love day and night in the mind and heart. Allow it to beat in the heart and rest in the soul.

"Fresh fall on me" is an intention that can help you surrender anything that is in resistance to Love. Focus on these words, allowing them to fill your spaces full. "Fresh fall on me." This opens the heart to new ideas, but be aware that forgotten memories may surface. If they do, embrace them as you repeat "Fresh fall on me." This position of awareness says to the Divine, "I am willing to have all resistance replaced with a new way of seeing– seeing through the eyes of Love I truly am." In this way, memories can pass through, as though a boat being lifted through the locks in a canal. So be it with the memories which are in resistance as they are being lifted onto higher ground where they will level out and go to sea/see, leaving only Love in memory.

Resist not this earth. Allow it to become a memory of Love. Herein lies the secret of opening the door to the kingdom of the eternal Love you are. So be it in joy as you place your steps upon the sands of the shores you are given to explore as you carry the attitude of "fresh fall on me." Let Love's unfolding be as a stroll on the beaches of Life.

Freshness of ideas flows freely through the soul that is open to freshness of ideas. Silhouettes shall come and go, yet you shall know the truth, for the Divine shall reveal the multi–sided complexity and simplicity of Love that you are. You are Love resting in my heart. I am your heart resting in your Love. And so, gather within you the unit of the transforming design of Love being "fresh fall on me," measuring it not.

Flow fresh with sweetness, children of Love. Your sweetness is your strength–believe it or not. So be it with you, sweet! Gentle arms become the strength of Love in earth. Allowing in nonresistance collapses armies which were strong in opposition. Holy energy fields rise as the walls of resistance surrender to Love's embrace. "Fresh fall on me!"

"Fresh fall on me" again and again repeat! Keep with this invitation in your heart throughout a day's time, and see what revelation, peace, and awe it brings to mind. Oh, you will feel sublime. The power of units of old shall fall away, and the measures of trying and trying shall be yours surrendered.

Fresh fall on me is an invitation to see life differently.

Fresh fall on me accepts all in memory,

Not just the good versus bad, but helps me see,

All is the gift of Love, so fresh fall on me.

Fresh fall on me is the sun's rise within the sunset,

As the Love of God moves within to forget

The resistance of mind to the unforgiven sought,

Remembering the Truth of the Love I forgot.

Fresh fall on me surrenders my mind

To the Kingdom of Heaven I've left behind,

To Love everlasting, to Love sublime.

Fresh fall on me, my heart's nursery rhyme.

Section Three

Love Re-members

Be the Love I am re–membered,

For you already be the Love I am.

Be it now remembered.

And here abide in

This realm this time,

Immaculately conceived.

As Christ the seed,

Be mine.

Chapter 11

The Is of What Is

When a vessel is empty, it is then available
for whatever choice is made to fill, and I,
the Love of God that created the vessel,
shall fill it full with the choice of
my own through you.

Questions rise, mysteries before your eyes. That which is to be understood is my yearning to know myself, for herein I *am* remembered. Thus I am empowered to see myself in all, which is the Love I am and my purpose for being. With you in mind, which *is* mine, I come to know the innocence of the child that Love calls to maturity.

In the beginning you are Love, and each design of Love becomes more of itself expressed and remembered, until finally all is forgotten except that. And in "That" you shall know yourself to be the Love of God I am. Hold me now holding you, by allowing–taking *no* thoughts of the mind to stillness. Simply rest as you would in sleep forgetting all, allowing dreams to come upon you. Each dream shall bring its own vision to help you know you are Love. I shall present myself in many ways until the day that I cannot present myself otherwise, because you shall know me as you.

No amount of coercion can persuade any transformation. No amount of begging can bring forth a changed state of mind. No amount of yearning can manifest goodness. No amount of force can persuade the heavenly realms. But your *Love* calls all I am into communication with you, revealing all you are to know. The center of you is where I already abide. Here, I am the Presence of the Divine you are.

The Divine is calling itself forward in acceleration to gather from the depth of silence the totality of being into one memory. This calling has become accelerated and is the gift to the soul that desires to abide in the Love tenure of the Divine. No amount of personal will can attract this calling to help you. Only the Love of the Divine, carrying forth *its* call from within the sincerity of the Beloved I am you are, can do that.

Glorified Divine is the Light that draws alignment forth in *this* world, and, at first, you may not understand this Light that enters into the chambers of the heart of the Seven Sacred Temples that abide within your experience in the flesh.

Nevertheless, passageways into chambers of the heart are being opened, Beloved. Resistance to the opening is like a mother resisting the birth of a child in her labor. Relax and breathe, for deeply is the One emerging, beckoning you to come close to see, to *observe* the Life emerging as thee.

Cocooned in your heart, if you will,

Beyond the mind's roving eye,

Is the butterfly to caterpillar kept,

That doesn't need to know why.

Your birthing is written in butterfly.

Your destiny is equally there.

Let the pains of your labor be still,

There's nothing for you to compare.

The crowning fortress of energy that surrounds the top of the cranium is a Light body unto itself within the Seven Sacred Temples within you. Here there is a release of power units equal to your Love vibration which accords itself within the name of the Divine. It is important to maintain frequency levels of love, joy, happiness, and peace of mind, which are the cornerstones for all other high vibrational energy tones within the body.

Peeks of information will flow. Do not try to understand them all at once, but know when they enter into the brain to give you wisdom, they will *always* remain. They will be there, accessible to you through your stilled awareness.

Focus often at the pineal gland. Keep the center of the Light there in holding patterns of stillness. Be not afraid to enter deeply into the cranium of consciousness, and be allowing to yourself in all thought that enters into knowing. Let not any thought become crystallized, but allow its free–flow as a river flowing in and through your awareness. Seek not to hold any vision other than "I am the Love of God." Let, therefore, your heart be pure. Let your mind be single in its thoughts, and feelings be embraced as peace and Love. Possess the Presence of the Divine as it possesses you. That which you are is already given–let it be revealed.

Gravity has a tendency to pull the human down. That is why it is important to envision, in the heart above the crown, that which is the halo of the Divine. This halo is not bound by gravity, but is pulled as a spiraling upward sphere by the heart of the Divine that is drawing your return to Love through the Seven Sacred Temples. Love energy is much more powerful than gravity in the pull of the Divine attuning.

Allow the energies to pull as willed

From Love itself as you.

The mind can float.

Allow it to.

Be still, my beloved you.

Locally, you will feel many changes occurring from every portal of awareness to which your mind knocks upon the door of consciousness. The heart of the Divine I am opens awareness like a feather floating into memory. And, as these portals or chambers continue to open, stand as awareness itself to the empty fullness that arises. Do not take anticipation to the portals' entrance, but sit still and let the mind frequency, which is forever increasing in the stillness of attentiveness, be that which releases and opens portals of the mind to allow you to enter these dimensional frequencies of Light. This can be done if you will open your mind to emptiness. When a vessel is empty, it is then available for *whatever* choice is made to fill, and I, the Love of God that created the vessel, shall fill it full with the choice of my own through you.

You are becoming purified in the energy chambers of your being. It is vital that, as these chambers open, they are not exposed to lower vibrations. Once they are filled with the totality of your awareness as pure Love and passion for life, then all other energies disappear, and you shall ultimately not be tormented by their content again. It is not as if they are pushed aside in you, but they simply collapse and remain so in the presence of Divine Love. Realize that the entrance to the portals of the Seven Sacred Temples within is *always* filled with love, peace, joy, and luminous Light. In their purified state, nothing passes through these portals less than these vibrational equals.

Love calls its own. So, Beloved, there is nothing left to do except answer the call. When you are called by someone you love, you respond. The Love of God is calling *you*. And, as you respond, you will ultimately understand you are being called by that which you *is*. The Master standing at the door is welcoming itself. The reflection you see is *I as you*. The one you call to is an extension of you, and the one that responds *to you* is an extension *of you*. *You* are that which you seek.

To the one being called, I am the answer within *and* the one seeking the understanding that is being given and received. Bring questions of your mind before the altar of the Presence which is resting as the voice in you. Herein lay the question to be heard in answered form, remembering it is I that bring the question, and I that fulfill the answer. No more questioning or wondering from a state of frustration, but a questioning and a wondering from excitement and joy, knowing the questioning and wondering is what brings forth what is to be understood in order to have a greater capacity for knowing. Mustard seeds begin to germinate as realized information and wisdom from on high. Is it not I? Yes, for I call myself forth to fulfill the desire in *your* heart to know.

There is no way to find God. God is not lost. There is no way to seek Truth. Truth is the Presence of the all–knowing Divine, and *you* are an extension and expression of that Presence. There is no journey to be taken. There is no mountain to climb. There is no path to trod. No god is left to find. There is only I to be. Do not seek. Allow. Do not be anxious about. Be with me. I am the Love of God you seek. There is nothing left to be sought. Instead, know I am the Love of God. Now, you say, "I am the Love of God." So, where is there to go to find what you seek to be the Truth?

You are what is forever you "now" as the Love that impulses itself to be true to what it already is. What you perceive as an urgency to *find* is the urge from the Original Design of you to be true to itself *now*! You will continue to feel driven to *find*, until such time as you are willing to turn within upon yourself and *accept* that what you seek *is* you and, therefore, found! Tell me, Beloved, what else could you possibly be other than an extension of the Divine? What gave you birth? What grew you? What beats your heart, digests your food, sources the earth, breathes your breath, falls in love? What learns and commits to memory, what fills the mother with child, arts itself to canvas, hears melodies unsung? What compassions your soul? Keep going–what reads these words? All that you are is the extension of the Divine. The Master teachers before you have all known this truth and tried in vain to convey the reality of union. But they have failed, for only union, which is already a given, can unveil itself. You are not something separate from yourself, nor are you separate from others same.

The joy of the Divine is in individuating the expression of itself. In many ways you are entering new fields of education with the *soular* reunion of these energies. Mastery is simply accepting and allowing Original Design to fully express itself in every individuation or situation of Life. Recognition of the Divine extended in *all* form will open you to greater revelation of its expression as *you*. And the ever–present design of mastership for many in this world is coming close to realization as unified circles of One.

Turn around and look at yourself everywhere and as everyone. You will see the Divine. Look not into another one's eyes and see *them*. Look into another one's eyes and see *you*. You are not separate beings except in flesh *form* only. The Life that brings forth flesh form is identical. In this truth you are your brother's keeper. Find your brother's keeper in the eyes of your brother, and find your brother's keeper in every aspect of Life. I keep that which keeps all, and to each is responsibility given.

Awakening as collective awareness is soon to make a big shift in what is available to become known. And, by the power of unified Love fields gathering here and there, many shall experience Unity consciousness or Oneness in the "twinkling of an I/eye." Trilogies of the soul–the seeker, the sought, and that which is drawing you–are one. Look to your right and to your left, before and behind, above and below, within and without. Find me there, for there I am. The reality of union will engulf you through recognition of "there I am, and there I am, and there I am, and there I am."

Let not the heart go seeking knowing.

Allow my knowing to be the showing

Of all reflection in Life I am,

Living Love returned as Source again.

Chapter 12

Eternal Life

*Widow yourself from all ideas that are
not true to Love. Seek to be revealed
as wedded into Eternal Life with
the Beloved you are.*

Such Love moves forward in this time. "Show us," says the hearts of those in assemblage. "Ah, yes indeed, yes indeed, show us!"

This message is about understanding the gift of Eternal Life–as is with all these messages, ultimately. For when you understand, accept, and live *from* Eternal Life, you know what is written in your heart as Original Design, and you live as that. You become fully realized, glorifying God and knowing yourself to *be* Eternal Life rather than "having" Eternal Life.

The Will of God invites you to embrace Eternal Life in the earth, realizing that Eternal Life measures not one plane to another plane to another plane and then again. No, no!

Eternal Life is forever, eternal, every single moment in every plane of existence. Let your heart be centered in this understanding and know the Truth that sets you free: I am the Eternal Life of God, NOW! The idea of death is so old. Let it be forgotten and forgiven. Glorify God by accepting the Truth that Life is eternal and, as such, so are you.

Divine Will is what is drawing forth the revelation of Eternal Life to those who are ready to accept and move forward in this gift. Divine Will, which is making itself revealed, stands in necessary abeyance until the will within you, Beloved, calls it forth. This is necessary in order for Life to recognize itself as Life and herein to call forth that Life.

Fragments of a dream simply remembered reveal the Essence of God forwarding its view of Eternal Life to each of you. Hallowed be the ideas revealed, and the Truth. Widow yourself from all ideas that are not true to Love. Seek to be revealed as wedded into Eternal Life with the Beloved you are. And the healing of the soul takes place.

The world in which you live is a world of Eternal Life. And such it is as that which is occurring in sweet earth, the wisdom center of my Life. It is not an easy journey in this plane, but trust it is an Immaculate Conception of Life, Eternal Life, and herein do I give birth to myself– companioned as the one you are.

As with Christ, the gift of Eternal Life is yours for the keeping, kept in you as promises written in your heart. It is a component of your Original Design and can not be altered or abandoned.

Surely, surely, goodness and mercy are filled with Life. Precious Life is given unto one in all from the same Source–the Source of Life I am. Holding fast that which is held by the Life of God in all, I abide. Herein abides the Truth: The Life of God, which is the all in all, continues to Eternal Life, fruiting itself of the seed of the Life I am. Herein you abide, keeping Love companioned with itself.

If you take the words of Truth and you hold them in a light, they will be the same in every direction. Herein abides that which is Eternal. For in that which is beyond the mind is the "Word" that speaks of what I am as the gift of Eternal Life, not known to the mind which understands and understands not, but from the heart of God that liveth Life within itself.

I do not come and go.

I do not rise again.

For I have always been.

The Eternal has no beginning

And it has no end.

Chapter 13

Cradle of Love

*There's no place to go to find me, for
I am with me as you all the time.*

No greater Love is there than Love itself recognizing its own in all you see. Find me, the Love *you* are, my Beloved, and know my gift unto myself is *you*. Coming from the heart is your deepest dream and herein written in all. Feelings from on high flow freely from Love in the heart, and so does my Love as you through which I create.

You are seeking to find that which is not lost but given, promised, destined, if you will, moment into moment. My Spirit is attuned with the Love of All. Everyone within my range is present with me and hears my voice speak its truth, for it is one voice in all. There's no place to go to find me, for I am with me as you all the time. The heart knows I am the Beloved. Let not the mind get confused, but rest in heart in observation to the Truth. From Truth, Love shall be remembered as the Divine.

Vacuums of the mind are cradled treasures in earth. Allow the mind to empty be, for here fullness rises for you to see that fields and harvests are one and the same. Vacuums create space for Life's creations to manifest. Behooves it not then for the mind to become the vacuum of the soul? Space is a container for the substance of Life, always seeking with openness by its nature to be filled. So does it not behoove the mind to become spacious? Does it not behoove the heart to become spacious? And does it not behoove the consciousness to become spacious within the container?

Let Love arise as the keeper of the Truth, and herein feel yourself cradled, resting softly, safely in your soul. Cradled as a mother's child in the bosom of the mother, let you be within me as that which I am you are, holding you quietly, softly, gently. And here you will feel nurtured as a child rests in a cradle, warm and safe.

Rock yourself as a child being rocked, allowing the rocking to be known as that which nurtures your soul of Love. Sit quietly, Love, and allow me the rocking to be gifting myself nurturing you. Rock–a–bye Baby in your heart is the nurturance that is sought seeking you. Come Beloved, let this be your lullaby silently within:

My lullaby,

Your song I sing,

Your Life I bring.

Trust this now, my offering,

My gift of Love remembering.

Rock–a–bye Baby

Your Mantra song.

Rock–a–bye Baby

All the day long.

Chapter 14

The Passion of Desire

*It is not the thought that manifests a
desired thing but the Divine
which sources the desire and thought that
manifests it.*

Coming into this World is a gift. Manifesting is also a gift. And each gift is the gift of the Divine as its expression of Life. Lovingly, what is given is received, and what is received is given by the giver and the gifted, one and the same. To those of you who have ears to hear, let all that is given now be received from on high. And let all that is received from on high be given again through acceptance by you, the receiver, activated by the ethereal loop of Oneness.

Desire in you is the passion of the Divine seeking an instrument of Light, such as yourself, through which it can wield its ideas and designs into manifestation. The gifts seeking to be made known are what the Divine would have you entertain as blessings from itself. Those who do not interfere, but accept desire as blessings being offered from the Divine and that they are *already* in keeping, align their energies of consciousness to the frequency of the fulfilled manifestation, thus glorifying the Divine.

If you would believe, what you believe will become. And that which becomes influences what you believe. Rest assured there is always a gift in either way, for they are both equal and the same within the laws of creation. Energy always reveals the magnitude of its equal in return. However, it is not the thought or belief that manifests a desired thing, but the *Divine* which sources the desire and thought that manifests it.

Doubt, fear and worry are disclaimers to the desires and passions of the Divine. These are the sins that keep one in suffering and also keep the Light from entering to bring forth its greatest glory, which is to reveal the passion and desires of the Divine.

When a desire rises, it rises *in* consciousness *as* content *of* consciousness, impulsing what is given and written in the desire that is *already* fulfilled in Divine Mind. There is only one way for fulfillment and that is through acceptance, which is *what* you *are*. Acceptance is not just an activity of doing, such as thinking or believing, but rather acceptance is *what* you are. Herein lies the secret of the Masters of ages old. They not only understood this principle, they lived *from it.*

Lift your heart to a place of total acceptance. When you can totally *accept* the desire from the level of yourself *as* acceptance, the manifestation is assured, for there is nothing left to *interfere* with it coming to fruition. If you resist in any way with doubt, fear, worry, anxiety, anger, resentment or withholding, then the desires of God cannot manifest their fulfillment. What *will* manifest is more resistant energies, for they are what is accepted.

Help yourself by being very still and looking toward the gift of God's holy Light of acceptance within you. Do not think on anything. Allow the mind to rest in acceptance. Allow your heart the same. In the rest, the Divine of you gifts you with the designs which draw you to themselves in order for you to become realized as the immaculate design you truly are. Here, at the center of acceptance, Eternal Light shines, revealing you as fulfilled in purpose and desire.

Passion is a fullness of heart and mind brought together in a focus of sincere willed intention. All desire rises from the original desire of the Divine to express itself as you in all your fullness–image and likeness. In this fulfillment, all else is added unto. And to God is the glory! Passion your heart with the desire and sincere intention to give of that which you truly are to the world, and thus to God. In that passion, the universe of infinite Life gives back to you more than you could ever dream. Stay open in between and all about yourself as you trust your heart desire to unfold. Let not your mind go to the rhythm of doubting as in the past. Be still, accepting and knowing your passion is in fulfillment now. Can you feel it?

Purpose has no meaning other than it is the gift that God would have manifest in earth through you. Open your mind and heart to your gift of purpose. Let that impassion you and be recognized as the passion of God to fulfill its nature and *unique* purpose through you as you.

When you understand this all–encompassing principle of Love, which embraces the manifestation of desire, passion, and purpose, you can easily see how all that manifests is God's Love accepted. Holding the Truth to *be* the self–evidence, what more could be needed? Wisdom teaches "seek first the Kingdom. All else shall be added." This is a wisdom teaching from the Kingdom of God's Love. This is a priority teaching of the Divine, encoded and etched in every being. "You are my encodement," saith Love.

> *To the heart's desires say,*
>
> *"Oh Lord, I accept,*
>
> *And thus I glorify Thee."*
>
> *This is the greatest Truth*
>
> *Written in your history.*

> *Embraced by the energy*
>
> *Of the eternal One,*
>
> *The Only Begotten comes home.*
>
> *Through you, children of the Light,*
>
> *I have found my own.*

Chapter 15

Here I Am, Lord. Use Me

True service is a gift of Love
and not a hardship of any kind.
It is what is sown in each heart
as the natural flowing of Life energy.

Mastery in Life embraces service, and each of you is headed in that direction at this time. Do not ever be afraid to offer what is service to every moment given you to live. And in the offering, that which is given is the gift of God you are unto itself. True service is a gift of Love and not a hardship of any kind. It is what is sown in each heart as the natural flowing of Life energy. Service ultimately becomes your pleasure, your passion, and your joy. Each time you gift service from a surrendered and joyful heart, you are automatically gifted beyond the service given.

Those of you reading this have more than likely felt this inner urge for eons. It has spawned the ceaseless prayer of your heart, "Here I am, Lord. Use me." Let it now be known to you at a deep level of understanding: The true nature of service rises *automatically* from the Love that you are. Service is a venue for you to be a contributor within the totality of the Whole of Life!

That which is the glory of God entertains itself with service. And, collectively, many are gathering according to the service needed and enjoyed. Let it be known you are all part of a global network of gathered beings of Love, each one complementing other gatherings of service adjoining adjacent. Complementary extensions of the Love within all beings constitute what is known as "service global mission." Many gather with you to complement this mission as you extend Love and Light through your desire to serve the same. Enter into this awareness and take your place among millions of millions. How many cannot be counted.

Gather strength in the numbers I have gathered. Empower one another with the Love you are. See only me everywhere. Presence evokes its own as the orchestration and the music of the spheres support the worlds within the worlds of service which I have created.

The Will of God at the center of your seeded nature is to expand awareness of the Love and Life you are, multiplied– complementing the Love and Life in all designs of form. You are about moving into a greater capacity of service at a Cosmic level, joining other beings of fulfillment and planetary systems of Light.

Those of you who are awake to the yearning of "Here I am, Lord. Use me," it shall be given. Prepare your body temples by purification, and hold open vessels of your mind by synchronizing intention in your heart with internal Will. Let not your hands do what your heart would not hold. Thus, a pure heart "shall see God."

As you continue to embrace your heart's prayer, intuitively you know:

> *This is the place I came to serve, and here I flourish as the Love and Light of God I am. Doors and windows are open wide, and all is accepted, provided–fulfilled!*

Be aware that any desire to be of service to the Divine is an invitation to be purified or aligned, which means you are willing to have many things adjusted. As this takes place, you may become acutely aware of false beliefs, resentments, or perceptions of any kind in resistance to Love. You will eventually come to understand they are the gifts of Love, bursting forth from any pain or suffering remaining as the effects of human will in opposition to Love. Ultimately, they shall be recognized and understood as the gift of God impulsing Love revealed.

The cross was made of wood.

The wood is but a tree.

Follow the Tree of Life.

Its roots are anchored in thee.

I am the Life, and I am the tree,

And I am the wood you see.

And I am even the cross you seem to bear,

The Life of God, everywhere.

Surrender all to the Divine! It is easy to surrender and trust as you stand beneath the Tree of Life bearing fruit of the past or current service. Be willing to move beyond your sowed garden into the field of Grace sown by the Divine, revealing new fruit, new fields of Love, and new dimensions of purpose, mission, and service.

Call my idea into time to express my fullness of joy, purpose, and mission that fulfill themselves in you. Whatever you love is my gift unto myself, breathed as the breath of Life of you. Passions of your heart are mine, drawing forth the gifted seed as individualized expression. Passion yourself to what you Love and *lose the constructs of your mind* herein. Feel my energy. Watch as the empty canvas of the mind receives images of my desire to bring forth your passions, your mission, and your work.

A potter molds the clay into an urn for water's keeping. Herein, a purpose other than the clay, but inclusive of it. And then the potter, who took the clay to mold an urn to keep the water, drinks. Again, a purpose other than the urn for water's keeping. One purpose is not greater than another, but always inclusive of all that is present. Be open to a purpose of service not yet fully known, but inclusive of all that has gone before.

The glory of God, situated within the purpose you seek, reaches forth with gratitude from itself to what it has created in itself as you. And in the energy called "gratitude," more of the service equal to the Divine Plan or Original Design unfolds to reveal the truth of which you are a contribution. You are here for a Divine purpose, a mission to complete, a Word made flesh in the heart of God revealed. Gratitude will be a feather in your cap if used fluidly. Watch the feathers of your mind drift slowly into rest as gratitude fills your heart.

Children of my beloved Self, can you see as you look into that which you are, my Presence? Sure you can. Propelling myself as though putting a small tube within a larger one, I stretch what is called "your soul." The frequency of Light pouring through this inner tube helps you forget what is no longer serving the purpose for which you were created. And it helps also to expand the conscious space of soul within you to contain more realization of who you are and your purpose for being.

Another view of the same effect is offered: There is a tremendous amount of power being released from within. Referenced as a "cosmic crack" opening a "black hole," so to speak, the Divine draws unto itself all entropied energies returning to the void from which they emerged. The continual drawing creates a collapse, complementing a stretch of the soul.

Children of Love that are gathering are experiencing a collapse of the veils of time which shall be no more. This movement creates cracks in the cosmic eggs of all concepts which have fulfilled their usefulness. It is a new world order.

Ultimately, you are the extension of pure consciousness in the presence of your own footsteps. You *are* Love gathered in your place. So, let it be, Beloved. Let you be! In order to assist you in *let you be*, visually place yourself into a center of Light, your Light body.

Bring your mind and heart to the truth:

> *I am the Light of the world, and I am strategically placed accordingly where I now serve. I trust that all Love vibrations of energy move collectively and have brought me to this place of service that is aligned with the Love of God I am and the gifts thereof.*
>
> *My contribution, vital it is, as is each participant in my circle of service. I complete and fulfill my design which complements all other designs of*

service. And, as I am gathered together within my circles, I am strengthened in my service of Love.

Caution: Love is the movement of God that impulses all change. Should your heart feel inclined toward moving or shifting, trust the impulse as the Love of God. Then open as you would your front door to welcome in a guest who has a gift for you in hand. Repeat your prayer, "Here I am, Lord. Use me." Then, if you still feel the desire to move forward and change, move with energy, *gently,* in a forward motion of pure intent to release anything in your life that continues to hold you in the space of service where you find yourself to be complete.

Caution: Let not your heart sink to an ebb which is called "doubt" should you desire a new place or gift of service, for herein the energy field wherein you currently serve is weakened. Functions may cease at your current place of service or relationships may shift because you are complete here. Always return to the prayer of your heart, "Here I am, Lord. Use me."

Pathways are made by those who walk them frequently. Be assured, a pathway is being walked by the virgin desire to serve that is impregnated in your heart. From this frequented path, your service opportunity that is contained within the Divine shall be revealed and fulfilled. And, as you faithfully await revelation of your next place or gift of service, you shall be at peace and trusting the eagle to rise.

Caution: Do not be dismayed or alarmed if things begin to close down for you in certain arenas of your life's service, for knowing now what you know, they are most likely complete. Complete your missions as assigned and, in their completion, wait patiently for the next. Let each day fill each hour with the knowing in your mind, "I am willing to complete the mission written in my heart this day." Your environmental shifts will be made clear and peaceful to your palette of desire.

Complete this phase of your so–called journey, understanding your prayer is right here, now, ready to be answered. Be assured, your purpose is revealed and your mission unfolded in greener pastures yet to come. You must be willing to abandon the past, release today into today, and receive tomorrow, here now.

As these arenas of service come to completion, trust your steps are guided, and your physical world is literally cared for in the guidance. Every step I take is yours is mine, Beloved, and all gatherings here and there are connections.

No place shall you be sent, any of you, that is not your perfect place of service. It will be drawn to you by the purity of your Love *expressed.* Also note: Your hearts' purifications empower you to serve from vibrations of your Original Design. And the day will come, and is rapidly approaching, wherein you will serve from a galactic measure, complemented by those in other realms equal to the Love you resonate.

When you sincerely desire to be in service to the greater plan other than self, you "merge," so to speak, with one another of equal vibration, downloading energy and information from worlds within worlds into earth Life form. Frequent your mind to the realization that realm to realm are your companions, and they serve with you what you long to serve. In every moment the mind allows itself with this truth, you will know you are here as Love and that you do not serve alone, for how could you when all is One?

From here to there is everywhere, and here right now I am. Thus speaks words of wisdom to what is the truth. You, on the other hand, sometimes forget and assume yourself to be a being all alone, abandoned by the nature of the Love that created you. That is not possible. In the space of alone, I am companioned by myself. Let all doubt or worry or even contemplation be as a drop of water evaporated into what is.

Be aware that hierarchical leadership positions of service do not exist in Cosmic realms. There is only the awareness of "I participate and contribute my Essence to the whole." The whole is what dictates leadership.

Keep with this desire to serve and let it be willed within the Will of God and the understanding mind to turn within to find its own. Here your gift of service is revealed. And for your friends who come to join in this, to which the service of the Divine is gifted, shall be the blessing equal. And they, matured in Love eons past and now ready to serve, shall gift the Grace of God and stand with you.

The Will of God now calls me to itself. I accept. I am the peace and the power of Love in service to itself. Completions, which I now release, empower me to move forward in the service written in my heart. I accept my place. I am eternally grateful in the service of Love fulfilled.

Chapter 16

Trust

*You cannot know by looking at the seed
what glory and beauty awaits, but you can trust,
that in the plan it takes your breath away.*

Trust is my activity within myself, spawned from what is true. The more you surrender and trust, what is true emerges. Without a *doubt,* I become a promise, *without a doubt.* Take doubt into its own grave. Eulogize it as a great teacher, but let it not resurrect before you as an image of reality ever, never again.

Daily as you sit in contemplation, trust that which contemplates. I am the Life of you–Source offering you infinite supply, tender care, flawless guidance, and unconditioned Love. Recognize I am everywhere present, omnipresent as Omnipresence. Recognize I am every power in the universe, and my power is good, for it is true to the principles of itself. I am all you could possibly desire–and more.

Trust as you would trust the bed to support you in slumber. Trust as does the spider to the web. Trust as you would the sun to rise in the dawn. Trust! Take no thought for the day– listen only. Calculations, indeed–let the mind rest from these and watch as fountains of Truth spill over into your life the gifts of Love. In this state of trust, gravitations of the mind synchronize with the beating of your heart and balance the system, whole.

Trust as the wisdom in the seed that knows the time to move and grow, drawn by the light of the sun. Every inch all the way is guided by the Love at the center of the seed, nurtured by the sun, the light, the wind, the rain, and all that earth contains to draw into expression the beauty and the glory in the seed. You cannot know by looking at the seed what glory and beauty awaits, but you can trust that, in the plan, it takes your breath away. Hold with reverence and appreciation whatever you see as the beautification and fulfillment I offer you.

My Beloved, pleasantries of your heart are many as you look at my world through my own eyes. Frequent often that which is beauty with an awakened awareness of "I am this expression herein being revealed." And the beauty you see as mine is thine. It is my call within myself seeking to be made known to you. Would you not accept and trust all I am you are, *beautiful* one?

Seeking is impulsed from what is already in being, like the flower in the seed to bloom, the lifting in the bird to fly, or the fragrance in the rose to give of its essence. But the seeking will not manifest your desire. Seeking simply delays the finding, for what you seek is here now. Your mind was created to think, not to see, and of itself it cannot *see what is true.* Only the Divine "I/eye" can see. I am the I of me, and I am the I of thee. You *are* the trust that *can* trust. Can you see? You are that.

Children come and go as authenticity, simplicity, and spontaneity. Let your soul be authentic as a newborn child, your simplicity pure in heart, and your spontaneity natural as well. Moment into moment is Divine, offering Life unto life unencumbered by doubt, fear, belief, or time. All is gifted in the moment from in all. Multitudes hunger and thirst for messages of mysteries revealed. How simple can it be to love one another? No mystery here at all. If there be one, it is how *not* to do that. That in itself is all the truth you ever need to know. Keep it simple as the child keeps the moment simple, attentive to what is in the play and the joy and the freedom of the moment.

Can you find me in the smile? Sure! Now you've found me. And what is it that makes the smile? See? To everyone's eyes in which you smile, look and see me. Every time your smile sees itself as mine, whether on your face or another that I keep, shall it be given in return. And know I am blessed within myself.

Many shall come to mirror yourself, but only *you* can feel and know you are the one you seek–accept this! In the morning's light, stand before the mirror and smile at me, and I will smile back at thee. You are the Light that is welcomed in as the Divine. You are the current reality of all Truth. You are the Beloved. Can you accept this? Then smile at myself in the mirror of your journey, and trust every step you take is mine as thine.

I believe and move myself to a new beginning in the day, a new rising of the Son in thee. Oh, my Beloved One, the I, I see. A mirror captures the image before it, but you are not the mirror; you are the image, I–am–age. And as the sun/Son rises to greet the morning waiting in the earth, am I rising in you, Beloved. Faces are turned to the sun/Son awaiting the rise, and with the heart centered in awe I shall be revealed in the "twinkling of an eye." Breathtaking is how you know me. Breathtaking! Pranamed before the "awe," find me there. Fortunes cannot be told that an "awe" keeps. You are that, my Beloved One. I've come to witness myself as you, and thus my joy fulfilled. And every time you feel "awe," acceptance *is* the heart of God as you. Trust and rejoice.

Greet each day with simple eyes and excitement for the unexpected. Feel the joy of knowing the moment is here to give its gifts to be enjoyed and to glorify the Gifter through you. I always gift from myself to myself, and whether you understand this truth or not, trust it to be so. Realize all I say to you is you saying all I say to yourself. And if you feel a resonance, a kindred spirit here, it is your own, my Beloved. All is available, all is complete, all is present now. Herein *be* my trust, for I am the Trust with which you trust!

That which is the only One,

The only begotten Son I am.

That which is to be

Is written in the heart of Thee.

Trust this, little ones.

Chapter 17

Source Serving Source

*You never do anything less than give of the
Source from which you came, back to the
Source to which you are giving.*

Glorified is God in Love when you desire to serve
Love in all. The heart opening in the earth, which
is guided by Love, is embracing many ideas which have
been resisted in the past. Each of you has resistances still
allowing. But now there is a greater capacity to open
wider the heart so that more of the entire universe can be
accepted, embraced, and laced with Divine understanding.
Resistance to anything will slow the process. Would you
resist the breath? You will pass out! But I will breathe in.

The world is a place of infinite creation. Eons of Life
have now awakened you to the realization that, as the
expression of the Divine, you abide in the creation of your
own choosing. The energy within the gift of choice is
coming to an apex, if you will, a point of new frequency
modulation, revealing that you are a conscious participant

of the creations of this world. With that understanding and acceptance, it is revealed that what has been created by you previously is now possible for you to re–create.

The matrix of design creates after the image of the mind, and the selection of the choice is equal to the design in effect. Every moment you have an opportunity window to be the expressed Love of God, reaching forth to make your selection of the effect the mind creates. The only choice you have is at the level of effect. Choose then the gift that has been given as unconditioned Love. That choice is equal to my choice within you.

Trust what is given is an equal measure of opportunity, and choices are yours to make. Collect information only for discerning what you would desire to have as entertainment through your choice. Your desire is to be entertained by the Love you are, so choose only what entertains you from that endowment. The eternal gift of Love is all that is ever and forever given as you. Ultimately you *are* that choice. *When* you make it is up to you.

Comprehend one thing–Love. From Love I source my joy. From joy I source my bounty. From my bounty I source my earth. From my earth I source you. From you I source my Love. From my Love I source all I am. Choose!

Suggestion: Look through the eyes of the created instead of looking at the created through the eyes of your sense of self. You tend to see an object brought forth in manifestation instead of letting the I that sees be seeing itself manifested. Focus on this truth; embrace this one.

As each of you more humbly and deeply accepts yourself as the creative Presence you are, the Master within you and those on–looking gather more insight as well. For as Presence is accepted by the mind through which Presence is unveiling its own understanding, that clarity is available to all through unity consciousness. Clarity deepens more clarity. It makes no difference which realm a being is living its existence, all receives and expands.

Like a river flows freely, so is the Will of God flowing freely. The gift of Eternal Life is the Will of God, and this gift flows freely from the Source. Think about earth. How many rivers are there? Where do they flow, and what do they supply? Such is the river of Life within your temple, flowing to all that is within you, nourishing, bringing forth the Life and fruit to which is coded in that which I feed. And so, as you recognize yourself as a river of consciousness, you will be able to understand the creative process at hand. For the river of Eternal Life being the Source out of which you, the consciousness of God, have come to understand the free–flow of Life, you now recognize yourself as the extension of Source serving Source as Life in all.

There is a flow that comes from the Source as that which you *is*. But it cannot be understood because it is the Source. When allowed with open mind, not thought taken of its own, Source fills the extension of itself you are, complete, and from that fullness manifests according to what Source contains. You are Love, and you are the manifestation of the desire of the Source.

As Source, you understand more of the free flow returning out again to create and to flow freely in creation back to the Source again. You never do anything less than give *of* the Source from which you came, back *to* the Source to which you are giving. This circular vision is rapidly awakening the Source remembered and saturating consciousness with the ability to understand, allow, and accept the free flow of creativity.

Herein, this leads to the topic of service, which brings the free flow of Source into the individuated idea or entity you call "self." Service is the purest expression of the free flow of the Divine when it is given without ideas of self. When service is given freely, understanding that "to give is to return the expression of Love to the Source from which it came," this activates a constant free–flow of substance to and from the one serving. In this return, you have what is like a battery charge giving more energy to the item which the battery charges. Thus, you have beings in earth, such as yourself, serving the Divine selflessly. In selfless service, that which has been created or given is free–flowing from Source to Source, serving Source fulfilled and activated again in the return from Source to the selfless giver–you! Thus, Source serving Source. A mind twister for sure!

In the past, much service has been given, but the service has been contaminated with the thought, "If I give, I shall receive." If I give, I shall receive contains within it a condition. And, in the pure free flow of Divine Love, there is no condition attached. Love flows freely without condition. Thus, you are encouraged to contemplate this dedication: I serve only Love, understanding that Love is without condition or end. In this way, as every idea contained within your individuation of the Self of God is brought to the understanding of "selflessness," you shall embark upon a frequency of service which is totally unencumbered–not limited in any way.

If you can grasp the gift within this truth, you will see that your expanded consciousness of giving shall return unto the Source a greater expression of what you understand to be the gift of Grace. Grace flowing into creation is without condition or limitation of any kind, and, understandably so, can *only* return unto the giver more Grace to be bestowed again.

Your Love for God has *always* been directed to yourself– but you may not have known it. For, from your point of view, you have understood it to be directed outside of yourself to God "somewhere." But, because God is all and omnipresent, and because you *are* of the "all" as the expression of the Divine, image and likeness, your Love for God registers inward within the Source of you, as well as the all seemingly outside of you. The beauty is that your Love for God is always *received* by you in the moment of the giving, even though, from your perspective or viewpoint, it is being directed outside yourself. This is what has brought your awareness to the understanding of Source serving Source through Oneness. The gift of Love always awakens the gift of Love within itself–Source serving Source–understanding, children of the Light–you are that.

When your mind understands that whatever you give is given unto yourself, a deeper understanding of that truth is revealed. In the giving of the Love of God intended toward others, you begin to see that others truly are yourself. And you expand to embrace all others with the realization: I have given to my Source. My Source returns unto me, for I am the Source in all.

This is what is expanding in awareness as the unified field or unity consciousness of all humanity and beyond. Joy is the frequency that concurs from the understanding that is born of one who realizes "I am all in All, and whatever I give unto all, I give unto myself." This is not a self–centered belief of the mind, but a self–realization of Truth that knows the joy of the experience of union. Nothing can possibly be given "just for self." And thus, the mind expands to embrace more of the true reality of God's design of all I am as you.

Transformation occurs when there is a transcendent look at things that are accepted by the mind. When there is a willingness to do that, a portal of awareness opens and makes it possible to transcend or transition what has been the previous understanding into a deeper one. Let, therefore, your mind be centered in *willingness* to release all concepts of understanding and beliefs, even though they have served you well up to now, drawing your mind into a progressive state of renewal. The greatest Cosmic Truth of the ever–unfolding wisdom of the mind is the willingness to release *from* the mind *back to the Source* that which has been given. Hang not upon "your truth today," for your truth today is designed by its own nature to expand and embrace more of itself.

Likewise, allow each thought that rises build upon what has been given previously. But do not insist upon standing and seeing what before you have seen, because, once a view is seen by the inner soul, it is ready for the next vision to be given. There are never two sunsets alike, and the Divine would have you see them all. Open wide your heart and the mind by simply willing to will the Will of God you are, understanding *that* to be the free flow of the Eternal Life Source that is you.

Have you ever questioned in the past? Of course, you have. Have you ever doubted in the past? Of course. The doubt is what has brought you to a new awareness or capacity to see a new perspective of the aspect of whatever you questioned. And so now, as you enter more deeply into this teaching, do not expect that aspect of conscious expansion to be different. The only difference will be a center point of knowing that, as you question, whatever the question may be is impulsed by the Source to reveal more of the Source as the answer. The need to understand through polarity is no longer the need.

Listening to the question is the first step and herein then rest, expecting and intending nothing but to listen to the question. As the question becomes the focus of the mind, the mind will turn in upon itself to reveal the answer, for always the answer is in itself the question–Source serving Source. And, as the question returns to mind a gift of knowing, then you shall experience an expanded awareness of Source.

Multitudes of gathered wisdom align themselves within you and read as though a clearly understood text–one principle building upon another principle in understanding–so that you have a pyramid of sorts to what is called "the single eye." At the top of the pyramid you can see it all.

Multitudes come to this understanding freely, as that which is the Source feeds that which is the Source, feeding that which is the Source within itself you are. Gloried be God in this truth revealed. When you glorify God, you glorify the God you are. "And herein you glorify God I am within all Life," saith the Divine. Do you catch this, Children of the Light?

Source serving Source, the gift of Love,

Unfolds its wings from Heaven above.

Revealed and healed as One in all,

My Love returns to Source recall.

Chapter 18

The Gifting

*Understood, this is a complementary
world of diversity, not to be diversified in
separation, but diversified in union.*

Seek not to grasp all that I speak, but to *allow* that which I have given myself as you. Enter into this, the realm I call my own as yours, by abiding in the willingness to be in Love. Love pours forth freely, giving of its own kind in measure, which can be measured not. The measure with which you now measure is to be forgotten, for that which is known shall take the place of measure. Life is not measurable by concepts which have gloves on. No, no. You must remove the gloves now.

The gloves of life give you hands–on information, protectively, so to speak. Now you must remove the gloves in order to feel what you thought you felt. Before now, your true feelings have been veiled by the gloves "at hand." Now you must reach forth and feel as the Divine of you. In reality, there is a feelingness of Light that can only be photonized, but you cannot grasp this, for it is not graspable. It can only be felt. True feelings cannot be grasped. They can only be felt. Take off the gloves.

Remove your veils, your shields, your gloves, and come unto me through the gift that is calling in you. Every time you *feel* your heart open to more, would it not be I who seeks to express myself through you as the more?

A Garden of Eden, if you will, everywhere, giveth I unto all Life. Each day brings into that garden *more* Life I have to give, for I am that which is the gift, the giver, and the given–continual. I know not how *not* to give. It is the same in you, yet you try at times to put a halt to the flow of giving which, by its nature, gives naturally. Abide in my givingness and allow free flow of that, and it shall be given you *all* there is to give–never running out.

I am the nature of who I am, as you are the nature of who I am. And here I abide as you, uniquely specialized, and each specialty complements the other to which I give in all. Understood, this is a complementary world of diversity, not to be diversified in separation, but diversified in union. Shoulder to shoulder I walk with myself–friend to friend, family to family, race to race, creed to creed. Diversity is my passion and my expression. And even I know no end to that which is called my seed.

Fountain of Youth, would you seek? Seek it not. It is eternal. That which is eternal cannot be found. It exists everywhere present, every moment, in every realm.

Fountain of Youth is the livingness *of* the Eternal being true to its expression of your true nature to give.

Fountain of youth flows freely from my Divine Life that is giving in every nanosecond. The giving of Life knows no end. It knows no beginning. Life flows freely as an eternal continuum. It has no choice but to replenish itself. In the replenishment of the giving of itself, you find the Fountain of Youth. To the giver who gives freely of all, this fountain overfloweth.

Love is about living *from* the heart of giving which draws forth the ever present Eternal that is sought. When Love is resisted by withholding instead of flowing unconditionally, this causes pain, suffering, disease, and even transition. Love gives Love because it can't help itself. It is its nature to give Love. It needs no reason. Rejoice in giving Love and feel it as it spreads itself forever young, gifting the purest alchemy of gold–the Fountain of Youth as Eternal Life.

If you would reduce a wrinkle in time, let there be joy in your face. If you would reduce a thought in your mind, let peace take its place. If you would reduce a weight in your body, let there be a "waiting" in your soul.

That which the heart tries to hold onto is not a giving, but a holding on. Paradoxically, the holding on becomes what is given. Focus: Holding on is not the nature of anything. Give and give again and give again and give again. And every time you give, I give again, receiving as I give, gifting others–receiving and giving equal and the same. Giving is the complete circle of the nature of Love.

Only Love carries its name, wholly and complete. It has no measurement. It has no boundaries. Expressions of itself are the totality of the whole, each a complementary part of itself. No more, no less, is equal to one. Receive what is given and understand in the giving and the receiving is the equal measure–no more value in one than the other.

Give what is given through the Life that giveth, and speed yourself into knowing by continuing to allow what is given to express, to hold not one idea or experience more valuable than the other. Collect your memories equal to the ideas of Spirit and register not one more valuable than the other. If equals equal, there is no conflict. There are no winners and no losers–no rights and no wrongs. There is only the Presence of the expression of the Divine.

When you resist, not with a valueless mind, then the Christ of you expresses from the manger state of innocence. The manger in your heart is the cradle of Divine Love. Herein your innocence is kept in a valueless state. My promise written in your heart is the equality of Christ consciousness in you, the child matured–adulted, if you will.

Focus more deeply. In relationship to *Oneness*, that which is given–mentally, emotionally, or spiritually–is received by all in the moment of the gifting. The all includes me, the gifter; you, the receiver; and all Life. Every thought, every emotion, every feeling, registers in me as you and simultaneously within the one to whom you give, as well as in all! Caution: This is true to *whatever* is offered in the giving. Do you grasp the magnitude of this truth?

Gift me not with things of earth, but gift me with myself, and thus all things are added unto me. The world spins in its own orbit. It has all it needs for support. And so do I in you, my Beloved One, as the orbit in which *you* spin. I hold myself holding you.

Powerful is Love synchronized as one, all abiding still, heralding from on high, below, within, each of you. And the presence of Presence gifts unto itself the One in all. As above, so below, hallowed be my name.

Taking me where I would go as you,

Would you not trust that I, the Creator,

Gift all you need and more?

And would I not gift the all

As I gift myself through you?

Oh, yes.

Section Four

Love Reveals

Return to that which is called your Life

With an awareness that it is mine.

And, as I am enjoyed herein,

Am I fulfilled by the sublime.

The Love of God I am is thine.

Chapter 19

Life's Lessons of Love

*Be complete with hide and
seek, and embrace
what was sought as found.*

Never before has such an opportunity presented itself from the Divine to behold the beginning of a new race. Consciousness is now in readiness to beget a new beginning, revealing Life eternal in all.

The Divine gives each day new with fresh ideas that unfold in glory. Everyone who aspires to remember to stay present in each moment shall be gifted with that aspiration glorified. Love what is given unto you to behold. Trust what is given is a life lesson of Love.

Collective measures of other incarnations support re–entry. Now gathering together as of old, strengthened by Love's remembered states, generations of the past have come again. Walking in the earth, they are united in a sphere of Light which gathers them in numinous space. Never before have the Beloved gathered in such multitude and strength–into a holding pattern of Grace, an impenetrable vortex of energy from on high.

Vortexes of Light spin, and spiraling motions are swirling dervishly. Mind rotations are multiplied and simplified. The Light holding you is the Light you are holding, and it beholds the Light in all.

Nature shall also be embraced and respond to this vortex of Light, and the earth shall remold itself, offering a new sphere of *presentness.* Envelopment of the soul of earth allows the energy field its space, absorbing, less resistant than the mind of humankind. Embrace the earth and feel its energy. Allow its silence to speak. So be it as your Source of wisdom's strength to add to what is offered.

Foreign matter patterns of old scatter and fragment. Fragmentations? Take no mind as does dust arising in the sunlight. Allow the Light to absorb the scattered. Foreign energies within you, not kin to what is Divine, are being tributaried, if you will, into Light. Let Light reveal all that is there to see, for far beyond what the eye can see are kingdoms to be revealed. And the glory of the Divine welcomes within you the Love which there abides.

Oh, my Beloved One, so close to home you are. The door is open. Won't you come in? Let us sit a spell and talk and chat, befriending one another, soulmates, if you will–one and the same, as dust returns to dust from which it came.

Multiplied energy fields collect with newness, begetting seeded ideas coded to the soul memory of Love. Beacons of God mind are a given unto you, spreading wide, as the holding pattern of Love intensifies its focus in the earth.

Love *for* you is all about the giving of myself *in and as* you. Your purpose for coming into earth herein is a blessing, a gift of golden light expressing itself as you. And your Love for others is a beacon of light spreading far and wide into the earth's atmosphere, unleashing gifts of golden light to all. You help me find myself in others as they stand before you, seeing only this Light, this Love you offer. Precious wonder, gracious Love, endless compassion, priceless joy, effervescent Light you will see.

Unencumbered by the mind, I shine. Understood with the heart, I impart. Captivated through the Love, I rest my case. You helping others is my joy, for it is the Life you are offering to myself in every One. See me there as yourself, as *everyone* yourself, equal.

Naturally, you will undergo many currents of energy that are foreign to the mind. Allow these currents passage. Beacons of Light come and go into passageways, measureless, as they are being infused by the Light. Do not question, for it is not for you to know, but it is for you to allow the Light to come and go. Divine Light is Divine Intelligence and frequencies itself aligned with Love. The attunement is attuning.

There are myriad energies for you to assimilate in your body temple. If you will pray with me daily, I will congregate them for assistance in your attunement. They have been given into the earth's atmospheric realms to assist the attunement of humanity and all Life. Naturally, things will occur that are foreign to what is known. Let not your hearts trouble. Oh, no, no, no. Not the heart to trouble.

Surrender all ideas which have unfolded through time, leaving empty space in the mind to be canvased with newness.   The measure to which you find yourself unfolding in Light is far beyond what can be grasped. Let not the measure be measured as linear, but know it to be omnipresent Grace.

As this Love–Light expands, it becomes known as your attuned individuation, and you are drawn to gather, multituding more Light, opening wide, portals of the Divine. And thus I gift myself aligned in quantum.

The Light of Christ moves in the vernacular, holding itself in tongues above and below. Correspond with your heart, allowing the opening of doors and inside chambers. Corrections beget unto corrections, and corrections correct again. Let not a troubled heart become what you know to be akin to Love.

Keep with the Love of Christ. Never look to other measures for measuring what cannot be. Correct the ideas of old information by implants of new regimes from the Divine.

Give the Light of Christ to all appearance for it is for all to be received.

It is not possible to grasp with the mind what is known in heart space. The knowingness of the Divine beyond the brain–mind exists forever in Eternity. So be it with remembered union. Forget it not. Fantasies of old pass away. Bridges are no longer needed. They have served their space. Collect not, nor pass over them again.

Reach with your heart. Focus with your heart. Allow the mind to rest. Stretch with your ideas to the only begotten of Presence. Be complete with hide and seek, and embrace what was sought as found. It shall be risen in the Love you are. Collect energy re–membered as "Oh, I am yes One." See it in all and behold it standing wherever you may be. "Never taken from granted," saith the Divine, "I love you."

Passage ways of holy energy are open, revealing new cleavages in the soul. Tumbling down through these energy fields, the cellular memory comes to rest in its purity, where it was in the beginning, Love. You are Love, and Love encompasses all.

No one shall be a sheep astray or lost or forgotten. You are all the extension of the Divine, and the Divine shall give you this day your daily bread and a smorgasbord of Eternal Life. Leftovers of the Spirit do not exist. Each moment carries its own fulfillment. Gratifications come in the measure of the gift given. Slowly allow that which is nourishment to feed. Try not to feed your sense of self. Remember, I am the shepherd and the sheep. I feed my sheep.

I give unto you this day. And every day shall be given unto you as it is. The blessings herein contained are not of tomorrow, but of today. The bread upon the table of the Lord, the house of Grace in which you live, accept with deepest gratitude. For I give this day daily bread which shall be nourishment in time. Let not tomorrow's bread be given unto you today–for it is not of the same essence and energy that shall be given once the bread given today has nourished the soul. My fields of grain become the bread, and herein are my children fed.

Fresh ideas as spring to winter's edge bring new Life. Say to yourself, "I will not hold on to yesterday's truth. It was sufficient unto itself to give birth to spring. My God, my God, I am remembering."

Trust what is given you to do. Listen carefully every day for my voice in all. I shall show you. I shall teach you. I am your voice. I hold myself in you now. Be of good cheer, for all is good. Let me take you where I will.

Never look past the moment.
Correct your time frames to zero.
Invoke your eyes to see with mine.
Allow the energy of earth to fill what is known as time.
Move forward in the heart space with the Light,
And remember, you are the Divine.

Chapter 20

The Presence

As the one and only Presence there is,
Christ is here always, for that Presence is
the Eternal Light that giveth Life in all.

Only the begotten of God reside in the earth, and each is my Presence–the Spirit, the gift of Love. This Presence recognizes itself, for time is nigh. Believe you are the Beloved, the Presence of Love energy as Light and Life. You are the Light of the world. You are the gift of your own Spirit. You are my beloved brothers and sisters. As such, I am impulsing my own idea, making itself revealed in your heart, soul, and mind, so you can know you are the Divine Presence, an extension of myself.

There is only one Presence, and that Presence as you is the gift of the Divine in itself. Recognize it is looking at each one of you as you are looking at each other, for it is the One looking in all. You are the gift of the Eternal Presence, the holy energy of the Divine, the Light of the world.

Let the frequency of the mind become *still*. Only in stillness can you hear me–only in the stilled mind. Take this idea into your awareness: I am the Presence of God. I *have* to be because I exist and I am here. My mind could not be anything other than God mind. What else could it be?

And, as the expression of God, image and likeness, the mind of Christ is here also as the Eternal Light that giveth Life in all. Christ is the fulfillment of the Original Design for all humanity in which you live, move, and have your being. Returning often to this truth brings your mind to its equal. And in Christ you know, "I am the Way, the Truth, and the Life."

With all children of Light coming to a greater expansion of Light, it is indeed a time of great change. Allowing is that which is called the Way. Wisdom is what is called the Truth. And you are what is called the Life, the Way, and the Truth. Truth will always be the center of the Life. Truth will always be the center of the Way. In the statement, "You shall know the Truth and the Truth shall set you free," is the Kingdom of God revealed.

Acceptance of this Truth gathers you wisdom and strength and gives measureless peace, joy, and abundance of Life. It lifts you out of "the mire" of the earth. It gives you permission by inheritance to claim your gift of absolute abundance in Christ, not from a sense of separation, as "Please, give me this, Lord," but "Thank you, beloved indwelling Christ in whom I live and move and have my being. Thank you, beloved Divine, Father in whom all is one. Thank you," and name whatever is your heart's desire, knowing it is mine in you to receive or give, embraced within the heart and will of the Father.

Jesus? Oh yes, "Follow me," to be sure, but know I am the one that gave you the idea to follow me when I said, "In that day ye shall know that I am in my Father, and ye in me, and I in thee." Follow me; know this Truth; be set free; lift above. I am in thee, thee is in me, and "we" *is* in the Father. There is only Oneness. Can you accept this, my Beloved?

Fathered of the Father is my birth as you,

Given unto sweet earth anew.

Again you've come returned,

Glorified by understanding the Love I am you are.

The journey bears fruit for you,

So, Beloved, be still and enjoy.

Feel full, satisfied,

Knowing I am glorified,

My Beloved One.

Chapter 21

Treasures of My Dream

*Your dreams are not your dreams. They
are the fulfillment of my treasure as you.
You are my dream fulfilled.*

Love is always drawing Love into expression, serving
Love. Fashioning the gift of your heart's desire, I
draw the Love I am into expression, and so it is. Revenues
from on high are as abundance flowing freely as an open
sky, filled with more than enough.

Pastures are green, Beloved. Feel the green beneath your
footing. Shed your shoes. Walk barefoot in the pastures
green. Double your opportunities. Rest in peace, realizing
peace is the absence of sacrifice. Peace rests and is ever
complemented by Love.

Quicken the fires of remembering as you affirm your
Essence fulfilled. Grapes are in season. The wine is new
to make. And the dew that is called to refresh the pastures
of morning Light I give unto myself for your pleasure and

the joy of knowing what is keeping all that is. Indeed, a gracious gift in earth herein.

Having created myself as the Love *you* are, my dream is fulfilled. Treasures of your heart are mine, keepers of the dream–equal and the same. Treasures from on high are here now. Open wide the doors of the Kingdom of Heaven inside, wide open. Heaven in earth is my dream fulfilled, and you are that.

Children of old have gathered here to serve, to love, to weep, if you will, away the tears of what has caused the sadness in weeping. Visions of Light, as stars twinkle in the blackened sky of the soul, await the healing Light to bathe away the tears. Even the farthest star feels the return of you, as Love be your gaze. And herein my heart *rests* as yours in openness to receive the Light in miracles of Grace omniwhere. Focus in the night beyond and see the Light yet to come, and yet is there, here, right now. As beyond, so it is–treasures of my heart. Make your wish upon a star. Become the child again and watch the dream unfold as mine, which is thine. To wish is to hold the dream of happiness I keep within myself as yours.

> *There is a song endeared to heart*
>
> *Sung by children near and far,*
>
> *'When you wish upon a star,*
>
> *Makes no difference who you are.'*

I am the wish. I am the star.

My dream come true is who you are.

Treasures of the sea are perceived as deep and hidden and to be discovered. Not so, my Love. Treasures of the *sea* are available now to those that *see*. *You* are the treasure of my own heart. Your dreams are not your dreams. They are the fulfillment of my treasure as you. *You* are my dream fulfilled.

You are my Beloved. Be loved in all ways in all days in all keepings of what is called time. My Presence is your own and extends itself through the hands of Love you offer to myself in another one. Welcome me home through the eyes and the heart that see the eyes and the heart of me as you observe myself in all. I love you, my Beloved. I am the Love that loveth *as* you. This is the only keeping that you have. And so the Truth continues to expand in awareness of what is true of all.

Herein I am the blessing given,

And you are the blessing received.

Sourcing from the Source, resourcing itself as you,

My treasured dream come true.

Chapter 22

Reflections of Myself

*There is no single other you
in all my universes.
There is no single other one
with your purpose for being here.*

From here to eternity I am kept within myself in all creation, and I abide in stillness as peace abides within the heart created I as you. Fathoms deep is the soul yet to be made known to the conscious mind. Be still. For herein as a pool of water do I show you your reflection of myself–in the still.

You are beloved, always, impulsed as the rays of Light of the sun from my Love. Love carries wisdom within the mind. Wisdom carries Love within the heart. Wisdom teaches wisdom. Light reveals Light. One walking in the state of awake, awakens all. Humanity is on the edge of awake, as a cat naps.

A wisdom teacher is one who desires knowingness. I am that in you as that to which you are aspiring. What is drawing you to wisdom is wisdom itself. Wisdom must be allowed. It is not manufactured from an idea or thought. Multiply your wisdom through wisdom. Rest and allow what is drawing to draw nigh unto you. It shall reveal in its own time what you seek. You are the wisdom of the Divine I am. Be still and know.

Coming together are large groups encircled, drawn by the Light–each one looking into the eyes of the other one to find me there. Herein I am revealed. I call these gatherings of my own, and will to will the Love I am expressed. Hungry are the children to be fed, and fed by the hunger is the paradox of Life.

Many are literally starving for the Truth that rests so silently they cannot hear. One keeping the silence empowers others to hear the silence. Listening is its tool, a powerful tool, spawned from silence such as fish embrace in water.

You are a participant in the Gatherings of Light, circles within circles within circles around sweet earth, rising bubbles of Love. Pressure not anyone to join your circles, but invite with open arms their Presence. Herein all is embraced by my Love, By my wisdom, and by my Truth.

Love generates from its Source far beyond the mind's conception of itself. Seek not to understand Love, but to be the Love you are, and herein will understanding be revealed from Source itself.

Watch the mind's movement generous. Watch its movement gracious. And watch its movement energized by its movement. Watchfulness as the engagement of Life is your pleasure and is the keeper of the flame of the Divine. Herein cometh ideas known that awe the mind, revealing images unto myself each day I live as you. Treasures of your heart are mine as you in I keep watch. And in the moments of precious remembering, I am always there, revealing more unto the watch. And in the moments wherein the moments rest, there I am as your heart's treasure. Watch as I be true to the treasure of you, for I have watched before through your eyes, keeper of my Love.

I can then see my ideas given, heralding from within myself, much like an artist sees when bringing forth to canvas or to stone or to clay that which is visioned within. It is the wisdom of all to watch the brush strokes of my Love canvassed upon your heart as I express my gifts of Life through you for all to see.

Every day is a new day dawning for you to experience your true Self and what you are here to give. Be still and listen for my voice to speak as your own, for my eyes to see as your own, for the Love that I am to reach forth in all activity to express. Let evenings come and mornings bring the light, and during the day be still. Activities need to be slowed, and inner activities need to be frequented for silence to reveal its treasures. Kiss each day with your Love–Light, and know 'tis I as you herein found in precious earth.

You are called by the yearnings in your heart to respond with *acceptance* at every level of awareness and beyond. Compromise not. Accept all! Refuse to refuse! You are so precious, needed, and loved as the Life expressing you. There is no single other you in all my universes. There is no single other one with your purpose for being here. Believe that and be true to yourself. All Truth spawns as new birth of ideas to be received, and herein am I blessed. Accept!

Cloud watching is a pastime of the mind. As you gaze within the clouds in earth, do you not find images? Indeed! Shifting winds change images. Shifting images change minds.

Mustard seeds grow mighty trees. These are ideas of mine. Hallowed be the ground in which I rest as seeds of Love and Light. Each of you is that seed, my idea, my prolific possibility of infinite expression.

Open your heart as the sprouting seed. Open your mind as you would open the palm of your hand to receive. Feel fulfilled as thirst is fulfilled by the pouring forth of living waters from the wells of Eternal Truth from which I rest in you. Capitalize only on what you Love. Let nothing be weighed as a greater measure than another. Balance!

Every day in every way be intentioned to no thought, allowing peace to absorb all that is contained within the mind, and herein there is fertile soil for my desires to emerge. Let your mind be a jury which is out. Take no thought. Simply rest, Beloved, and be fulfilled in earth as you–my mind, my heart, my wisdomed Love.

I love you, each one, beloved of God, points of Light within myself. Return to earth mind consciousness from Heaven's Light state of awareness, and be the joy of the Lord, equal to the One. With Love, go in peace.

Captured in your Essence,

You are the effervescence

Of my Life, my Light, my Love.

My mind, my body, and my soul,

You are the mirror of the whole,

A reflection of myself in all.

Chapter 23

Resting

Be at peace, and in the peace all that is perceived
as need takes a rest from itself, thus allowing
fulfillment to be your voyage of pleasure.

Very often the children of Light have fears that are difficult to release. These fears are bound in consciousness, much like what is trapped in a spider's web collected. It seems impossible to untangle what is trapped in the web. Let not your heart trouble; there is a way. It is the way of Love through peace. Be completely open. Take no thought. Rest in listening as you read.

Only peaceful movements of the Divine can spread a wave of melting energy strong enough to separate content from the bondage of the web of consciousness. The entanglements of the mind must be alchemied, transmuted, and changed. In your deepest center you realize this–an elixir of peace is necessary. But how to find the elixir of peace is another story. Yes?

You, Beloved, must learn to rest, like Moses in the basket, allowing the river to take you where it will. It is impossible to get lost in the river, for the river always flows to the *Source*, and the Source *is* peace. Divine Mind draws forth this elixir of peace, carrying its will and its mission as soon as you crawl into the basket and *let* the river flow you to its Source.

Divine Mind always works through you as you. Taking a river cruise enables the mind to *be*–empty, still, soft, no hurry, just being empty. The fullness of my Presence rests in your heart and can only be brought to the surface as you rest in me. Peace is like floating with no resistance. To resist is to sink and to fall. Not to resist is to let me carry you, to float and stay above, to always stay above.

Consider peace as the sky rests within the heavens above. Gift yourself with cloud watching. Watch my images come forward and disappear–no mind, no resistance, no care, or concern. Sit in awe of sunset's beauty and be at peace as the day softly disappears into the eve. Be at peace as your breath rests between its inhale and exhale. Be at peace as the ocean rests within its shores. A swing moves in directions opposite. Find the point at the center between the up and the down. Rest there. Simply allow the rhythm of the earth, as the tides, to pull you in and out of activity–giving and receiving, taking no thought, just giving and receiving. Be at peace, and in the peace all that is perceived as need takes a rest from itself, thus allowing fulfillment to be your voyage of pleasure.

Here, Beloved, rest awhile.   Allow as the tree does the wind and the storms and the seasons to pass it by.   Resist not.   Flow as the ebb of the ocean's shore to keeping in the wave, here and there, in and out, and in and out again. Ebb and flow, life does go.   Rest!

Let there *be* the peace that is, as in the twinkling of the stars, and herein is the rest you seek fulfilled.   The realms beyond this one open wide, entry to the heart, and the Master teacher is called forth as your own.

Wonderment is a joy within the joy you are, and, as you rest in wonderment, joy is revealed! Rest often as the sun rests in the Light.   Rest often as the mind rests in the keeper of the mind.   Rest often in wonderment to these things! Present your fingertips to silk, and you will understand the feeling of rest on the physical level.   Then watch the worm spin silk from itself, and you will experience wonderment.

As you continue to unfold the peace of you, Life expresses itself beyond what appears to be.   It moves much further than the expression expressed and goes forth to bless the region it opens for you and others.   So, my Beloved One, rest.   Like the chords on the harp, once they have been plucked—rest! The music continues beyond the pluck given and is received in the galaxies far beyond.   The Divine is the one and the only song.   Its melody of peace plays in the heart of each, bringing together the orchestration of Life.

It is written in your heart, "The Presence of Eternal Life is *resting* in myself." Resting in myself gives birth to new beginnings. There are only new beginnings. There is no end, only new beginnings. Herein do I rest in peace.

Wishing wells are of the past,

So rest your mind in mine at last,

As butterfly whose wings are stilled

And hummingbird to nectar filled.

Chapter 24

The Stillness of Stillness

*Progressions of the soul
are not measurable in time,
but in the peacefulness of the mind.*

With you, abiding still, is stillness. It waits as the spacelessness of space, and herein am I found, remembered. Calculate not life with that which is thinkingness. Let my Love be the calculator, and you take no thought.

Understand that evolution of the soul continues in a spiraling motion of opaque openings. Progressions of the soul are not measurable in time but in the peacefulness of the mind. Peaceful thoughts spawned from pure Love, let them flow. And, as they flow through you, you will begin to know peace is what you are. Reduce your thoughts to a grain of sand, one grain of sand–allowing. Allowing all to be what is in the moment, time stands still, and herein the mind is kept.

Be stilled by the stillness I am you are, and herein you will see me always. Infinite *is* infinite and always eternal. Stilled awareness is the pinnacle of the infinite eternal position of Love. So be still. Be still and know. Be still and know and hear and believe and trust what you hear. Let the mind be so still that in its waiting it becomes the stillness in the waiting, and stay present. Accept all that is present in the moment. Focus! Be stilled by the stillness that you are. It would benefit no talking for hours, staying present and accepting of what you find in the mind. The more you resist what you find in the mind, the more in the mind you will find to resist. Watch every movement from eyelash to foot–walk. Let no thought put asunder the Eternal Life that is watching and Truth be revealed herein.

Gracious is the movement of the eyelid to the objects before it. Watch yourself as the eye of the I rests upon what is there to be rested upon. Humble surrender allows all that is present to be what it is and nothing more or less. My Kingdom is come in the freedom of what is accepted without judgment or identification. Sturdy endurance to focus allows purity to navigate its journey to bring Truth to conscious admiration. *Focus now on focus.*

Most are hungry for the truth given as perspectives of ideas of truth relevant to the embracement of Life in earth. Truth is not a perspective. Be stilled *by* the Truth. If you are not stilled *by* the Truth, it is not Truth. The only Truth there is, is Truth itself. And one who keepeth "watch," which is *still,* aligns with Truth, equal and the same. Truth is only known in the stillness of itself. If multitudes were to gather in the way of stillness, Truth would be revealed. Allow the beauty of this message given to be in lingering.

When prayers are ushered from the stillness of the mind, hope and belief are not a part of the movement herein kept. Hope and belief are phantoms of the opera that slept. Be now awake to belief's curtailment, for herein faith is the elixir of stillness *found*, beyond belief believed. When belief deplanes, the only Truth there is remains. Truth needs no belief to be what it is.

No more belief.

No need to.

Rest in what you know to be true,

And let every thought be "I love you."

Politeness is indeed the gift of unhurried, synchronized energy of the mind. In stillness, one energy introduces another one, not crashing into, but introducing–deeper and deeper, higher and higher frequencies. Steady as the sun streams into the earth be your focus.

Energies rising, spiraling, spinning. Trinities of soul merging to one. Holy ground herein you rest in waiting. Let reflection be a token of what is offered by what is witnessing. Take no mind to that position. Rewards are given in the stillness of the waiting–as the One is stillness waiting upon itself found. A seed cannot reflect upon its making nor its breaking open to proceed its gifts to the garden. You are the seed of my Love in the garden of my Life.

You have come to the garden, the waiting place, the stillness of the mind. The breath is moving in and out on its own accord by the Love of God I am. Let the movement of the mind be as automatic as the breath. Let the breath of Life carry you to the fulfillment of your Original Design.

Let your evenings become more frequent in the passion of stilled silence. Gather often, be still, and wait in silence. Be aware, I am here, I am there, I am omniwhere. You *are* the stillness of stillness. Be still!

Let your desire be to still the mind and let all else come into that desire, and all else shall be given. Experience yourself as silence. Be still and know. Be still and know and hear and trust what you hear. Be still and allow all to be.

The Beloved of all that Love keeps

Is shared in silence deep,

Aligning heart–soul memories,

No more the soul to weep.

In silence attunements atone

In the caverns of the soul.

Its wisdom reflects memories

From silence to behold.

The Love of God, heart renewed,

Its silent mysteries shared.

Allowing is its motive

From its silence everywhere.

Chapter 25

Empty Fullness

Desire with your heart,
not to understand, but to be
re–membered as understanding itself.

Those of you welcoming this message understand that harvest time is here. And, with rejoicing in the soul, 'tis time indeed, for the journey has been long. So, come now to the banquet table of life, open and receptive to the Divine ideas of God's Word from the councils of Love within yourself.

Lovingly, your abiding faith, which has grown as a mustard seed grows a mighty tree, gifts itself through you and accepts what is at the pentacle of faith to manifest. Holding patterns of the past are weakening in the soul. Each *concept* of reality is being challenged and shattered. At the same time, fields sown in the past from the heart's Love of the Divine, come forth rich with harvest for your soul, and bless you with what is offered. The fields are ripe with harvest now, and with open palm in heart, receive the fruit, offering others equal and the same.

Joyfully, that which is given be received. Joyfully, that which is received be given. *You* are the mustard seeds of my Love. *You* are the sower of my seeds. Mustard seeds are sown and guaranteed to reveal what is not seen in the seed by the naked eye, but they contain, nevertheless, the miracle of a mighty tree. In you am I such a mustard seed as thee, Beloved.

Yet, there is more to be given and received than what you harvest today. All the gifts of Spirit you now know have filled you to capacity's knowing, and new gifts to harvest are in waiting to fill your current occupied space. Therefore, let there be emptiness of mind, like an empty cup waiting to receive.

Mother Divine is giving birth to new–born seeds of innocence and multitudes of deepened understanding. Your part in this delivery is to keep inviting yourself to rest between your breaths and know that Mother Divine is drawing forth new Life and unfolding new understandings beyond what the mind now holds as seeds of truth. Relax and breathe, observe and receive. Measure not what is given, nor even try to understand. Let understanding reveal from itself.

The essence of Life expands itself to knowing and grows stronger with each breath. That Life from on high descending, that keeps you entwined in Love, was seeded in the soil of consciousness in the beginning and now sprouts, as accepted by you, the soul or soil in keeping. The purpose of this expansion is to remove the shelled parameters of mind and encasements of bondage in the heart.

Planting soil sounds like an impossibility, for where would you plant the soil, except in soil's keeping? Well, this is the way of what has taken place with Love–a planting of Love in the Love of God you are. You question: Where do I find the Love I am? In the Love you are, of course. And osmosis within the Love of Love you are now Graces remembered union within mind and heart.

As Love rends the veils, parameters, and encasements of bondage from within the mind and heart, let it be known this is a second coming from Christ consciousness–a brand new awareness far beyond what the earth would keep in knowing. The heralding of The New Age? Oh, indeed. That was pabulum compared to what is taking place within The Golden Age here now.

As this Age intensifies in purpose and experience of purpose, *let* your heart be opened by the Original Design of Love as you. Take no mind thought. Wait in emptiness as fullness rises. Let it be as though mastership has hallowed itself in name, becoming realized as One–understood only *through* understanding *as* understanding, soil planted in the soil of consciousness. No amount of coercion can seep wisdom and understanding into your awareness. The

Divine itself is determining momentum, speed, and what is experienced as timing and readiness.

Energies fill, infuse, and defuse interchangeably that cannot be understood. Questions arise that cannot be answered. Recognize this to be the impulse from on high, knowing that, at this stage of your evolution, understanding is the result of a questionless mind. And with each question, let the mind cease, period, end of question. Rest. New way.

Carnations are a gift of Life, as flowers to the soil. It is a coronation, if you will, crowning upon your head the flower of Life, the understanding of the Will of the Divine turned in upon itself revealed.

Packages of information will be dropping into awareness systems in this method of understanding. Let them be unwrapped by that which is the timing of Spirit. DO NOT open yourself!

Trust what has been and is being given, and know that Spirit has and does carry you as wind to a leaf to where it would rest awhile. And let the entertainment of the day be in the resting joy of Life, penetrating through veils of time remembered and allowing the energies to conform to what they are designed to be and do.

The gift you will be *seeing* is an understanding that will empower you to simplify the most complex of systems or situations. Your awareness will be as if each system or situation is segregated in the mind, understood in its entirety, and known as to how it functions as a whole. The Master teacher within is Divine Mind that empowers you to embrace this field of awareness, and nothing shall be excluded–absolutely nothing. Yet, this is not an activity of mind, rather awareness as the Truth which sets you free. And it shall be effortless to you, for it is my Presence in knowing, from Truth.

Help yourself help yourself by being still and listening as was the way before, but this time do not go and try to open the door! The handle shall turn by itself. Allow what is discovered to come within and sup awhile.

Envision, if you will, a flag attached to a pole, the pole attached to earth. The flag is at rest. The air is still. Herein waiting, keepeth I, myself in you. And, as the wind bloweth, the flag begins to move, not knowing from whence the wind cometh. This is the only frame of reference to take to each moment in time or each waiting. This will take practice, however, understand one important fact: The only way to practice is to *allow* that which is practicing to empower you in *its* way. And so it is in keeping with that which is *empty fullness.*

Mustard seeds I sow through you.

Empty soil receives,

To harvest fullness omniwhere

As empty fullness conceived.

Section Five

Love Abides

You are my practice and my pleasure.

You are my breath and step I take.

You are my awake and my asleep.

The Love of God

In every moment do I keep.

The promise written in your heart abides.

Chapter 26

Already Fulfilled!

*Hold not a vision of a dream, but allow
the dream to be given and received in
its fulfillment according to what is
already complete.*

Understandings come and go within the capsule called the mind, and every turning of awareness begets a new understanding. Trust what is offered here to be the equal and the same from every position of awareness.

You are discovering you no longer yearn as much to be loved as you do to *Be Love*! This is a true sign of awakening and attunement. Being Love, you love to love for no reason other than Love is who and what you are. When that is your discovery, you, the child of Love, yearn more and more to find more to love, as if discovering new flavors of ice cream. When the love to love becomes your passion, new laws of creation come into play, bypassing an intricate system of mental constructs. As awareness of the Love you are surfaces, it effortlessly reveals its flowering, gathering in the gardens of health, happiness, deed, abundance of all opulence, and glorious relationships. Love one another as the eternal Love where you stand. Seek only to love from the balconies of Heaven within to be given–not from the need for reason, but from the true nature of your being.

As the love to love deepens, listen carefully with your heart, awaiting Love to impulse, guide, speak, or reveal. Wishing wells pale in comparison to the living waters at the depth of true Love, and hungry are the children to receive from their own well the fulfillment and gifts of Love's keeping.

Wishing wells, oh indeed, many here today. Wishing wells of the heart are precious indeed to the individual who thinks desire is one's own idea. But desire is *not* one's own idea. It is the *I–dea* of the Divine fulfilling what is already fulfilled in itself. Sourced from Source, the water flows the gift of Life. Draw freely, my Beloved, from *yourself*, and herein be fulfilled, the water full. Your wish fulfilled 'tis mine, 'tis thine, one and the same, Source serving Source.

A helping hand does not mean "a doing for," but a steadiness of companionship on the journey of Love. Softly, feel the heart begin to open, an Open Sesame if you will, to a deepening experience of Love–an experience of *being* rather than trying to *find* fulfillment. I am the lifting and the freedom, the Light, the journey, and the soul remembering all as One. Your journey's fulfillment is assured, for I am here as you right now. I am the journey of assuring your assurance of this truth. Hallowed is the keeping of your destination here now! Punctuation marks in a sentence give emphasis and clarity. You are a punctuation mark in my Book of Life, creating an adventure and a journey all your own.

One cannot capture this, for it is the Essence from which all flows. If you will be still, you will see with your heart, not your mind. I love you, my Beloved. It's that simple. You carry me everywhere you go. I carry you–one step, one step.

> *The dawn contains the night,*
>
> *But it cannot be seen.*
>
> *The night contains the dawn,*
>
> *Equal and the same.*
>
> *Children flow in their play,*
>
> *Taking no thought for the day.*
>
> *Pastures green, fields of gold,*
>
> *Multiply in every living soul,*
>
> *The will, the work, and the Love I am.*

Lovingly, I am offering you what I am you are, now. True spiritual advancement constitutes "circular" movement as graduations of the heart, wherein nothing is lost and nothing is gained. As spiritual advancement expands, what is revealed is that only what is true remains when all else deplanes. What always remains is Love being Love, Life being Life, Wisdom being Wisdom, Truth being Truth, and the Divine being the Divine–YOU! The Divine exists not in a differentiated state of a sense of self, but from the wellspring of the eternal Presence it is. You are That. Yet, you long for it–why? Your mental constructs inhibit awareness of the Truth revealed here. Mental constructs not in alignment with what is true are like a virus in resistance to wholeness. The virus spawns a *yearning* for wholeness, as wholeness seeks to be true to itself in expression as the nature of the Divine.

Our Father–one and the same, the eternal name of Love– offers Truth from within itself, and, as you rest here, all is given you to know beyond the constructs of the mind. Circle after circle after circle complete spiritual understandings of Truth, like bubbles rising from a wand. It is the Divine, the only One, being true to all that is. And, thus, the law fulfills itself as the Grace–full movement of Love–being you.

As the Word, the Truth, is heard and lived *from* and given preference, each of you–one, two, three, millions, billions–is coming into the ocean of *seeing*. This is the Immaculate Conception, the birth of Christ as rebirth in the earth, giving its Life through all. The Word now reveals its assurance and is a welcomed joy of embrace.

There is no more coming and going. There is only being to be. There is no path, no way, no journey to walk. There is only my voice, my Life, my all in all. Let the words of my inner voice speak loudly to your heart. They are easily discerned by the frequency of joy that is felt. That which is known is given. Holy be these words unto you. Take them as a gift of Grace, and let not your eyes move away from these teachings until you have engaged their totality and are truly accepting of that which you are.

There is only Wisdom, Truth, Love, Peace, and Joy. There is only God, the Divine I am, and *that* as all–Love, principle, law, matrix, essence, oneness, differentiation, worlds within worlds, moments, omniwhere, and gifts of Life. All is fulfilled resting in fulfillment–to be shared, given and received, equal and the same.

Hold not a vision of a dream, but allow the dream to be given and received in its fulfillment according to what *is* already complete. I live my Life as you. You live your life as me. There is no begetting me, understanding me, finding me, believing in me. There is just I that Be! Accept, accept, accept! How can you not? How can you not?

Let it be known this Word speaks of and from its own Source, and it is revealing its own Source every time there is a surrendered state of acceptance within the circle of humanity's spiritual advancement now being completed in the soul of individuated you. I raise the wonder of it all. I am the fulfillment of the wonder. I circle myself in dreams, designs, and truisms of Love within that which is longed for. All *is* fulfilled. And when *that* is known to be the Truth, the I/eye shall see only me–omniwhere.

It is as if you have arrived at the Equator, the center point of the earthly heavenly experience. All is being balanced. And in the balance and the equilibrium, in the allowing of all Life to be as it is, there shall be a frequency rising from the essence of Source serving Source as you. It just is and will be and has been–no name, no word, no experience. The mind doesn't like "no experience;" that's the nature of the human, but the heart thrives there, my Beloved.

In the realized state of the One I am,

There is such a greater plan

Than I, created as man,

Can understand.

I the human have come again,

Seeking to know what God commands.

Choosing the Love of God I am,

More is revealed of the infinite plan.

Chapter 27

The Attunement

And the day will come, and you will know,
Love is the only do to Be.

As the Declaration of Independence, you are that, dependent upon all independence, equal and the same. Your mind, my mind; my mind, your mind; equal and the same. Significance is the beholder loving itself in all it sees.

Cascading as waterfalls drawn by a force into the earth, such am I as living waters of Truth pouring in and through you. Your Love cascades waterfalls and touches all pristine and pure, calling it forth. *Feel* and *know* what you are, believe beyond belief, as a mountain climber's faith and trust.

Packages arrive filled with Grace. Let them open one by one. These are treasures far beyond the mind's comprehension or ability to understand. Love holding itself always gifts what it is beholding. And in the surrender and accepting of all that is given is that which is received–I love you. And in the heart, the flame raises gratitude–an open door, once more coming home, the children I am you see.

Multitudes are gathering gatherings in recognition of Oneness in each individuation of the Divine, serving one another an orchestration of Love. No longer one by one to be awakened, but multitudes. And herein find the glorified and call me through. "Come, Beloved, I love you." Let this be your voice spoken silently. Let it be known, the children are coming home. Not one by one, not two by two, but by gatherings of multitudes, this I promise you.

Multitudes attend that which is the gift at hand. And that which is loving is loved as the same in the one standing before you, whatever the name may be. You *are* the multitudes, followed by the "the," the "that," the "it," the "at," the "when," the "why," the "where"–all begotten of the Son of God, loving one in another as one Life. My heart is so filled as you realize: I am that Life. And I am blessed beyond my own measure to comprehend or convey what I love so much as myself as you. What a way to live and be remembered as such, experiencing that which I am. Indeed, could I be more blessed? And will you allow me, my friend, to be yours? Precious Grace this Life.

I love you, Beloved. Let this be the gift unto you known and forever to be shown. I stand with you as with all. Your heart is mine, brother/sister to me. Friend, indeed! Hallelujah! At last, at last, someone to whom I can speak freely of myself. And, as I sit side by side and hand in hand, I experience myself in everyone.

Love me now as I love you in everyone you see. And let the program be unplanned as the morning to the evening's smile. And love and love and love again until you think, "Oh man, oh man, what shall I do with this?" And the day will come, and has, that you will know Love is the only do to Be.

You do not come and go.

You simply flow,

In precious moments, like a baby's smile,

not knowing why or how,

just knowing Love.

Chapter 28

The Golden Age

*Perfection is always the end of the
beginning and entropies back into that
which gives forth the seed to begin again.*

The Truth, which is freedom, gathers strength and momentum, and the world arrives on time. Place not your attention in elsewhere but now, so that all that is contained is revealed as given. Further not the ideas of understanding, but those of being present as the *nature* of Love.

Opulent universes within worlds supply the need and the demand of universes created from within myself. Each species of I–dentities is my Divine, expressing realm to realm, universe to universe, world to world, connected as the home of a spider's web. Movement within the web itself, at any juncture, creates movement in the entirety of the whole. Therefore, remember, Beloved One, your Love is the movement that affects the whole. How important then am "I" within myself you are!

Strategies no longer work. Information systems no longer support, having fulfilled their purpose in the past. New structures unfold, new commitments, new desires, new wisdom and understanding as to fulfillment all unfold. Each of you is a vital piece/peace of the puzzle and complete within yourself.

Wisdom follows you as you follow wisdom and teaches from itself. Love follows you as you follow Love. And the Master within comes forth to proclaim, as Christ, the day has come that I know myself to be the Love I am. Thus I glorify God. I see myself where 'ere I go, and I dearly love myself. Sculpture yourself, etched in the eyes of you, as you look at me looking back at you in others eyes.

Holy energy is manifesting through you for simplicity sake for generations to evolve. And that which is glory beyond the mind's eye will be gathered as more fields for you to entertain and rejoice in, in worlds to come. God never ceases creation of its own extension, and every extension which fulfills its purpose is empowered by collectively uniting to create a greater extension of the Divine so that every mansion is more glorious to the beholder that created it. And the Holy Light of God, which measures not itself, let it not be measured by you.

With the Love I am in you, the world is yours for the accepting. Understand the Word you have been sent to speak is empowerment, for in it contains what is remembered union.

Congratulations, each of you. Graduations have passed. Portals and passage ways into the unknown now await and call. Return often to the space you know as peace, and herein wait in stillness as the flower in the seed. From the depths of the sea of consciousness do I rise and herein feed my soul as your own with wisdom, love, and understanding. Words pale to describe in any reference or literature as to *how* this takes place.

Each sunrise is a new beginning. And that is what I stand for in the resurrected state of myself. I am the risen. I am the Divine, risen, awakened to a greater dimension of myself, and yet each dimension is perfect–ever the same, but always blooming into greater expression of that which was the same before. Perfection is always the end of the beginning and entropies back into that which gives forth the seed to begin again.

I am the risen One in every heart,

In every child I awake.

And I stand before you in the dawn of the day,

Awakened from a lesser state

Of knowing I am the Son of God

As you, the same.

And for you teachers, behold this information now as teachers of old. Allow the children to listen to what I speak through you, humbled from the heart by eons of

Love being true to itself. See me looking back at you as students of the fold. Holding candlelight to one and only One, offer wisdom. See it in their eyes. I am wisdom there. Listen to my voice as it comments to you the question brought unto the floor. Know within it contains I, the information and the answer I hold within them. And so shall be that which you desire revealed. I, as teacher and the sheep, follow thou me, humbled. Ah!

Lovingly, the gift of God returns itself to your awareness, and you shall expand in that which you are known, to incorporate the all. The Love of God then gives you a new opportunity to serve in another dimension where your gifts of individualization have orchestrated a communion. Your awareness of the power of God to reveal unionized individualization is needed. Your mind cannot understand this process, for the term "individualization" and "union" do not mesh and seem to contradict. However, this *is* the paradox of the attunement and the spiraled–circled effect of incorporating all geometric design, individuated and unionized. All shall be known as Oneness and individuation within that Oneness. As to how, that remains the mystery of Grace.

Treasures from the far fields of the future worlds will begin to opportune themselves to those of you in rediness to receive. And the return of Christ consciousness in the earth, prophesized by minds tapped into future generations from the seed of the original collective design, shall unfold rapidly in resonance to the peace of Christ.

Galaxies beyond and universes within assist you in the calling to draw in–ward. All *is* being drawn inward and feels sometimes as though disappearance of the inward or outer life that used to familiarize your mind is taking place. This is true at the level of conceptualization of belief systems and traumas of soul memory. Love is purifying virgin space in consciousness for your mind to embrace the fulfillment of the revealed Divinity and Truth of you. Praise God and the immaculate of Grace.

I, the Christ, abide at the center, assisting in clearing and guiding as your heart opens even more deeply to the tune and womb of Life embracing your soul. I am the awakening unto itself from the darkness, allowing time to give itself time to advance awakening in time. You are all awakening in time, out of time, at the same time, in no time. A time spent is a time spent. Press not against the walls of time, but allow them to crumble on their own.

Given in time you shall see I am the risen. I always rise. It is my nature to rise. It is my nature to lift. It is my nature to begin again, to come to a new beginning one more time in earth. Every day is such. Every moment in time is a rising, a drawing forth. Forever young I am. Remember this. There is no death. There is only a drawing forth of Life.

I am forever. You are forever. Life is forever. Life as Life is your life–my life. And I continue to arise. Just as with each new day, I rise again and shine my Light upon what is in the earth multiplied.

Create an altar in your heart, *not* as before for the purpose of surrendering burdens of lifetimes, but as a gift of the Love you are accepting yourself as being. Come not to the altar to relieve your burdens. Come not to the altar with intention to sacrifice. Come not to the altar with a sense of letting go. Come to the altar as the Love *you* know you are. End of it, my Beloved. End of it as all your burdens collapse in the face of Love. It is truly the beginning of a new world–The Golden Age of Love!

Light is a beginning. There are photons of light everywhere, and, as each light wave unit moves in assignment, that which is written emerges. At this particular time, all light photons are coming together to express Oneness. And thus you have what is referred to as "A New Beginning" for all photon Light wave beings. You are One. And as this Light expands, all is affected and returns to itself. Loving one another now, move forward in this new beginning. Allowing is the secret of all time. Do not force. Do not resist. Do not try to understand. Allow is the secret of all time.

Cosmic energy moves deep into the spaces of time. And that which is the motion of the energy to give forth a new birth in this world speeds its motion as each heart and soul returns to Love. Present not anything less than Love in the earth. Accept not anything less than Love in your mind. Receive not anything less than Love in your heart. Extend not anything less than Love in your life. Love is the immune system of all dis–ease. Love is who you are.

The beloved Jesus, the Master whom so many follow, gave unto the earth the equal of these teachings. And He promised, "In that day you will know, I am in my Father, you in me, and I in you." As the Master within you continues to unfold and reveal this truth, can you accept the fullness of your Divinity? Your *acceptance* is the greatest gift you can offer. It is the ultimate gift to the Divine written in your heart and the heart of humanity.

Come, my Beloved, and follow me.

It all began in Galilee.

Returned to Love your Oneness be,

Accepting your Divinity.

Chapter 29

Becoming the Master

Can you stand before the mirror of yourself
And behold the Presence?
Can you love the Presence with all
Your heart, mind, and soul?
Can you accept that the Love with which you love
Is mine, and mine is thine?

Can you accept you are an expression of
The Presence of the eternal Christ,
And you carry within you the same power
As the Master teacher, Jesus?
Can you allow this power to come forth
And embrace all that is,
Giving and shining the Light
Through all, in all, as all I am?
If you can, you shall become a Master
In a short amount of time.

I am the Light of the world in all,
And I bring unto all a gift—the
'One' who stands before you in each individual.
It is my Presence within them that comes into your Light,
And your Light that comes into theirs.
Can you love them as your Self,
The Presence of Love in them as you?
If you can, you shall become a Master
In a short amount of time.

Can you, in every single moment,
Behold My Presence standing before you in all?
Can you, from the gift of your Spirit,
And the mind of your Spirit which knows this truth,
Find this truth as it looks out through your eyes?

Can you return unto those who take
That which you would have yourself receive?
Can you be the giver and the bearer
Of good tidings to all,
No matter what they may do or say unto you?
Can you embrace all these things, My Beloved?
If you can, you shall become a Master
In a short amount of time.

The power of humble adoration
For my Presence in others

Will bring to you the greatest expansion
Of the gift of Grace in your heart.
And that one who stands before you,
Expressing the least amount of my Light,
To that one, if you can give this gift,
You shall become a Master in a short amount of time.

To the one who calls you by a name not so loved,
If you can find my voice in all that is spoken,
You shall become a Master in a short amount of time.

And to the one who bites the hand that feeds it,
And you be that hand which is feeding the little one,
Can you say to this one, "I love you"?

And to that which your eye at first does see no beauty rest,
Can you find it here in all you see? If so,
You shall become a Master in a short amount of time.

And some of you will be guided to take up your palette
And all that belongs to you and move away,
Or change locations, or occupations.
Can you do this in faith according to the
Instruction of the voice within your heart?

And can you lift your heart above
the sadness of the earth
And the energy you sometimes feel when you rise?
Can you lift your mind and heart above this energy field

And hold the joy of the Lord throughout the day?
If you can, you shall become a Master
In a short amount of time.

Harmony is the gift of Grace,
And it runs through you as though a lifted bird
Singing its heart into my Presence.
Harmony is the gift that unites all in harmony.
Can you hold the harmony of Love
All the day long—no matter what?
If you can, you know the result—
You shall become a Master in a short amount of time.

Chapter 30

The Emergence

*Allow the resting place of mind and heart
and body and soul to be in you a time for
the metamorphosis of Life itself
to begin a new alpha.*

The Master Teacher of you emerges as do butterflies. Overnight they spin their cocoons in silence as they merge with all I am drawing them to be. That which crawled in earth now flies free and boundless, not even remembering that of old it was the earthbound caterpillar crawling through life.

The beauty and the freedom of the heart comparable to caterpillar and butterfly–Ah! Do you think a caterpillar in the earth could understand the freedom the butterfly feels in its being? No! It must experience it first. A time of cocooning in the earth is about the children of old who are tired of the long and arduous way, the many feet that press upon the earth, the steps of this before that and that before this. Allow the resting place of mind and heart and body and soul to be in you a time for the metamorphosis of Life itself to begin a new alpha.

By and large, seeking time is over, Beloved, for seeking takes the mind to journeys that cannot find what is not lost. Open your eyes to where you stand. Behold the holy ground is where I am you are.

As I accept myself as the gift of Life given, I behold the Divine I am in all, and I am humbled by the gift given. In that receiving I give again, returned to Source. For I constantly gives of itself, no matter what the expression of that may be. Ah!

I, the lover of all Life, am the Life that is loved. Within me I sit myself abreast. The galaxy within begins a new expansion from which I inspire remembered union with my Beloved Self in all dimensions. And here I unite with one unto the One I am in all, a greater realm of Heaven keepeth in myself.

There is within the belly of the bird the knowing of freedom in flight. To that which is free it rests in the belly of you. Know yourself as freedom's gift to Life. Soar with me as I soar in you as the Soarer observing the earth to which I have sent myself in you. Take dominion in your heart by allowing that which is in earth to be all it is in me.

Working with the lifting on the breath of Life which carries you above the earth and yet within, soar you now to places yet unknown that are drawing you home. And in your soaring, sing *your* heart song as that of the bird from the totality of the Essence of your being. You are the song of God.

Vacation yourself to peace, love, and laughter, deep and long. Then feel the smile as I sit within the song that Love is singing you. My voice is yours. It sings your song, whether verbal or not, to all who cross your path. The song is sung from within. The Hallelujah chorus, the silent voice of the choir of God remembering itself, realm to realm, rejoices as your voice. My voice in earth I sing through you. I hold the note. I am the song. The music of the spheres complements that which is all in all. And the sparrow sings with equal joy without remembering. Trust the balconies from the soul of Love to capture as the singing dove the one and only Truth I am you are. My voice is yours. Accept this truth.

And remember this, Beloved: The symphonies of your song blend with the symphonies of the song in all. And herein is one melody kept individually, a multitude of songs singing–one choir, one voice, one song.

The Love of God is the Word that is living through you. Allow me to speak myself through you as the wind speaks itself through the leaves of the tree. Allow Life to rise in you as sap in a tree. Allow the Son in you to call forth what is within the seed of Life you are. Rest in the earth, your feet grounded in the sands of time, your heart pounding on the shores of what is beyond, yet to be known. Explore this world as anew. The Kingdom of God herein is given. That which is sought is the son, the daughter of God to be revealed of its Light, incomprehensible to the eye that stares the object of its sight. Rest within Light's baskingness and allow it to penetrate. Thus, it sees itself in you returned as the holy energy you are, walking in the sands of time.

Focus with your heart on whatever idea is given you to know. From afar, what you desire shall be drawn near as you behold the Divine in all. Know and see: I am the Life of all there is; I am the Love of all Life; I am the Light of the world, the darkness of the world, and the Light that shineth in the darkness. I am the only begotten son or daughter of the Divine; I am the Master in everyone; I am the spacelessness of all space, the timelessness of all time, the Eternal of all eternalness, the wisdom of all wisdom, and the infinite of all infinity. I am the creation of all that comes forth from itself. I, the Love of God, eternal elixir of Life, am forever in the One to which I find myself, in whatever form I be. All that I am is you, and all that I have is yours to behold and be–holding. Trust me now.

The heart of gold awaits its alchemy, now to be given in the world to come. Stand in that which you find Love, for it is the fortress, the protection shield of all that before sought to break through the armor that had no breakage. The armor has collapsed. Your freedom is forever. Your gift is priceless and cannot be verbalized. So it is with the Love of God you are. Hold steadfast as Love in earth, and you shall emerge as One re–membered.

Far beyond what you know to be, the new world awaits. You believe the world to be what you believe. Believe it to be more than can be believed, and thus you shall conceive as gifted, Heaven on earth.

My Heaven is here.

There is nothing more near

Than Heaven here.

I walk in it as you.

And all it takes is a tiny seed

To be revealed as true.

Chapter 31

In the Beginning

*Eternal Life, not known to the mind
which understands and understands not,
is the willingness to reveal Love beyond
comparables.*

Listen carefully, every word. Listen carefully. Care–
fully every word. In The Beginning: In the beginning
was the Word, and the Word was without form. I reached
within myself, and I said, "Let there be." To become that
which is and the world within to hear, the Spirit spoke
the Word, "This is the Will of God. So be it in the earth.
Let there be Light." And the Light begot all that is to
become and all that has unfolded of recognized idea. And
in the Light, the Light said within itself, "I choose to be
that which I am, LOVE"!

And the Word, the Love of God, desired its movement as it
perpetuated the idea to Mind. And Mind, upon acceptance,
revealed the instrument and the channel through which
it is served. And the I accepts with "yes" of mind and

heart. Yes!, be the only focus of your mind; Yes!, be the only focus of your heart; Yes!, be the journey of your soul, Beloved. Everlasting is the everlasting Love. Into this awareness keep the movement of the mind still.

In the beginning was the Word, and the Word was the Light given, and the Light given was the Love received. And it became flesh in the earth bearing seed equal to the Word. You are that. And the Light unto the earth gave birth unto all it contained and found itself to be the Love of God as you. It kept coming from the earth until it energized a point of awareness–to behold that which is within itself, which the Light is, and reveal what the Word said as, "I am the Light of the world."

Understand the Word to be the image of the Word being you. In the beginning was the Word, and the Word was with God, in the beginning. I am the Word you are. There is no separation or idea of such, and there is no *other* you.

The center of your heart is filled with Light. That Light is called "The Light of the World." The Master Teacher claims, "Ye *are* the Light of the world." And from this center, "let your Light shine." If you are reading this, and you are, your passion is to be true to this Light in all its fullness. What is offered here is the way of Grace in the revealing.

Mind is being bathed with its own Light. And here is where you begin anew, for in the beginning was the Word, and the Word said, "Let there be Light." I trust myself to be that which is given within me, for I am all in all, contained within my–Self. And I hold my Light as the gift of the Divine. And I again began again within the Divine, the Word made flesh. I carry forth my Word upon the land to which I have come. And here I shall receive what the land would give unto me. I shall give back unto the land that which I perceive. And the Truth shall be given unto the world, and the world shall offer the Truth within that which is the world itself.

And from on high, those who are begotten in the Light of God return to serve the One. How many times have I begun within the Divine again to behold more of the Word in the Truth which is the Light! The Light carries every seed which I am. I behold myself in the gift of the Word to give again, and so it is in earth. Far removed from this time shall be the given at the speed of Light– multiplied more than the speed of Light is giving itself even now.

For I am the Word,

And I have said, "Let there be."

And into that I have spoken

The all of eternity,

To unfold, to gift, even I to see.

For I am the gift of God,

And God is the gift of me.

∞

The wisdom from above

Now herein hear,

As I carry forth my Word in you.

And in your times of peace,

Where I can speak mine,

You shall know that I am thine.

∞

And if you listen carefully,

Your voice to be mine

Shall be the gift in earth.

And all time shall here consume

That which is the Word,

Embraced within itself again,

Holding Love.

I believe in that which is faith, for faith is given in the seed, and I am trusting the seed to give forth what it contains. For in the desired given is faith revealed. And here the faith begins a Word made flesh anew. Trust that which is and all given unto you.

I am your Love. I keep within myself each other's heart; I hold within myself each other's Presence; I reveal within myself each other's Truth; and I keep within myself each other's precious Light, which is, "In the beginning was the Word."

Beloved, each of you, from which the Light now shines and the voice from which the Spirit speaks, is the One I am, and you shall know yourselves by what is found in the Word as you, holding your Light.

I shall speak and softly energize what tomorrow brings, carrying you safely into the gateway through which I swing myself as you, the peace of Christ. Simultaneously, the moldings, if you will, fall away, and that collapse giveth unto you something more comparable than peace. For in what is beyond the mind and words spoken is the gift of Eternal Life.

Eternal Life, not known to the mind which understands and understands not, is the willingness to reveal Love beyond comparables. But if you take your *thoughts* about Love or Eternal Life to be the truth of these words, then you cannot know their truth, for your thoughts are always based in comparables.

Your Love, measured not, reveals the Love of God! And soon the mind shall know it is not known of itself, but simply an extension of the Light which is an instrument. Beyond the mind I rest myself as the Eternal of the all I call you now to know. Serve what is the known in you to be a gift expressed, so you, too, can knowingly reveal what is–the Love of God made known through the Word which is as you. All is rested in the Word which is given in the heralding of the Divine.

And, I, the keeper of the Word,

Am the beginning, the alpha and the omega,

And the beginning again.

Such it is as the Love I am.

I am the Light, and the Light you are. Trust the Light which is given is the trust you are welcoming as your own. And you shall know the Word by what quickens within. Hold the Light of Truth, "The Light of God I am."

Joyous movements of Love are embracing you. So is my breath to the world. If you will take the breath and allow it to be consumed within to focus upon, it shall reveal to you the secrets of the worlds within.

That which is the Mind consumes all and allows its regeneration to pass and to collect with new Light. The Light which is collected is given unto the world a new beginning. So be the Light of Love.

It is the Will of the Divine that you rend all veils and step through the portal of The Golden Age which is the seeded. You have fulfilled what the seed of Love has brought thus far, and as you gather more of the fruit in the earth, you shall seed and seed again the new world order.

Your fields of joy are coming to a place where they can be sown again, and the seeds that are being sown are of a new generation. Total tranquility is the gift in the seed. A deepened awareness of the Presence of Light in the seed contained gives its energy to what you are, so that your mind can come home to the re–membered state of union. You will then be a participant as well as an observer, and you will understand mysteries revealed.

I am Love, Peace, and Joy. I am the gift of the Word of God and the Life made flesh in all. I am the Spirit from on high that gifts one with the understanding of the mind. I am the Light of the world. I am the Divine!

So take what you have as the mustard seed

Of the faith and the truth and the wisdom from above,

And allow it to sprout its wings.

And here ye shall soar in the Mind of God,

As Heaven on earth it brings.

And holding forth the willed idea

Of the return of the One,

So it is with the Only Begotten Son.

Fill yourself with the realization: I am the Word of the Divine, and that which speaks through me calls forth that which is gift. And that which speaks through others calls forth that which is gift. I am the Presence of the Divine called within itself as the gift of the Word made flesh. I am the Word, and the I of me made the Word into itself as me. And as the Word, I now gift the Life of earth, and in the Life of earth I set myself free to be and to love and to produce. And I have done just that. I acknowledge that it is the Divine that giveth Life as I. I am the Presence and the power. Now say that to yourself, and you will feel the truth set you free to *BE* what you are.

> *Have you ever been the Light within "I"*
>
> *Which calls you to that which it is?*
>
> *Oh, indeed! For this is all that is.*
>
> *And soon the mind shall know*
>
> *It is not the beliefs of content,*
>
> *But an extension of the Light*
>
> *To which it is an instrument.*

Reasons are not of the future. Memories are not of the past. Gracious movements of Light are all the I is, and the unfolding of that to return, to be, and to express. I is the Presence of all Life in existence and the Source from which all Life emerges as I, the gift and the giver, and I, the giver and the gift. Name and claim your heart's desire, for truly it is mine, and speak the word, "Thank *you*, oh Lord I am you are." It is like Light finding its own light which it created, to reveal it to itself, to take it to itself, and to give it to itself. So *be* this, Eternal One.

Let these words be remembered as written in your heart, the living Word of God. And the power to ascend to their Truth is the Love within the Word here written. Listen carefully as does each note in the symphony waiting upon the next one in the stillness of itself–*before* it is sounded. With Love, go in peace. As Love, be the Love you are.

"Let there be,"

To gift the world beyond the mind to see,

To be experienced One in all Eternity.

To herein golden world I bring,

The Light to re–membering.

The speed with which the Light now flows

Shall be multiplied a hundredfold,

To be the gift of Love returned,

To gift again Divine Sojourn.

Diadra is the co–founder, along with her husband, John Price, of *Wings of Spirit*®, a not–for–profit foundation dedicated to expanding awareness and awakening the Original Design of the human Spirit within humanity.

These messages were received from the realm of the Cosmic Christ, accessible to all through the Oneness of Love Consciousness. The Word made flesh is thine own.

For speaking engagements, workshops,

and retreats, contact:

Wings of Spirit ®

e–mail: wings@wingsofspirit.com
website: www.wingsofspirit.com